CW01021305

# SPORT

## AROUND STOCKPORT: THE EARLY YEARS

## THE FIRST STOCKPORT MULTI-SPORT HISTORY BOOK

FIRST PUBLISHED IN GREAT BRITAIN BY
SIMON MYERS, 'PALM BANK', 43 ELMLEY CLOSE,
OFFERTON, STOCKPORT, CHESHIRE SK2 5XE

© SIMON MYERS 2009

ISBN: 978-0-9560067-1-4

Printed & bound by
Fine Print (Stockport) Ltd.
Unit 6F, Lowick Close
Newby Road Industrial Estate
Hazel Grove, Stockport
Cheshire SK7 5ED
Tel: 0161 484 2244
www.fineprint-stockport.co.uk

# Introduction

The first two books I have written had been purely on the subject of football - 'The History of Stockport County A.F.C.' and the national history of the game, 'Football The Early Years'. When I told friends that I was planning to compile a publication covering ALL sports, there were doubts I would achieve my ambitious goal! **There has never been a Stockport multi-sport history book written before.**

I received an excellent response from various sports clubs in the Stockport area about their early history, and soon realised that I already had a very good framework for the project. Many of the sporting organisations had achieved their centenary and produced a booklet to celebrate the event - also providing me with some excellent 'vintage' photographs.

I always knew I would have to spend a lot of time at Stockport Heritage Library, in order to find the 'complete' story of sport via the old newspapers stored on micro-film. I viewed a total of 90 volumes of papers from 1822 onwards and have the eye-strain to prove it!

I have always lived close to Stockport - Cheadle Hulme, Poynton, Marple and now based with my wife Jean in Offerton. In view of the football coaching I received at Hulme Hall College, Cheadle Hulme, I should have 'made it' as a professional footballer. Our Sports Master was Trevor Porteous, who played for Stockport County for many years and was later Manager. Ian Greaves, a great character, who was a player for Manchester United as a 'Busby Babe' and was manager for Bolton Wanderers and Huddersfield joined the school for football training, plus Ray Wood (Manchester United).

I played football for Poynton briefly, whilst living there, having been 'spotted' playing in a friendly on their ground. Having moved to Marple I turned out for Mellor in the Lancashire & Cheshire League - always somewhere in the forward line. I also played Squash for several years, plus some table-tennis.

My most successful sport, however, was cricket. I had joined Poynton Juniors on leaving school and had just been picked for their 2nd team before the family went to live in Marple. There was an excellent team at Marple Cricket Club when I joined as an opening bowler, but within 4 years I had won the 3rd, 2nd and then 1st team bowling averages. Initially the club played in the Lancashire & Cheshire League, which allowed professionals, before becoming founder members of the Cheshire County League.

My father took me to watch Stockport County around the age of 10, and I soon became a 'fan' watching the team home and away - still a season ticket holder! I also follow Manchester United, and used to go to Old Trafford in the days when Best, Law & Charlton were playing - when you could pay and walk in on a Saturday afternoon!

Enough about me and back to the book! The **earliest recorded sporting event dates back to Stockport Horse Racing in 1764 on Great Moor.** In the first part of the 19th century, this pastime attracted the largest sporting crowds. There were Racecourses at Cheadle, Bullock Smithy (Hazel Grove), Heaviley and Wilmslow.

During this period, **betting on sporting activities was commonplace** - foot races, sparrow shooting, cock and dog fighting, anything basically!

The **first mention of Cricket appears in the 1830s at Churchgate, when the game would have featured under-arm bowling!** No doubt the sport will have been played in Stockport before these times, but crude in nature! Throughout the 19th century the 'class issue' raises its head in several sports, no more so than in cricket. In the 1840s, there were 2 main clubs in Stockport - **one for 'Gentlemen' and one for 'Tradesmen'.** This trend followed for many years to come within clubs themselves, even when these 2 clubs had folded by the 1850s.

We trace the history of **Stockport Cricket Club** founded back in **1855.** The various grounds they played on - the touring **Australian Cricket teams came to play in Stockport in 1878 & 1880** - the **famous W.G. Grace** played in the United South of England X1 v Stockport's 22 men in the **1870s**, all at their **Higher Hillgate ground.** We see how local cricket clubs 'sprung up' all over the area throughout the 19th century.

In the 1870s to the 1890s, Rugby dominated association football - most parts of the Borough possessed a rugby team. The **original Stockport Rugby Club** started in the early **1870s** at Bramhall Lane and became founder members of the Northern Rugby Football Union (later the Rugby League). A very early match report is shown of one of their matches. The first rules of the game encompassed the **'Rouge'** as featured in the formative years of association football. **One of the first ever rugby games played under floodlights was at Cale Green in the 1890s.**

The 'round ball' game started to grow in the 1880s and by the turn of the century, rugby was in the decline. **Stockport County** evolved from members of Wycliffe Sunday School at Heaton Norris in **1883.** All the **founders of the club are listed** plus a profile of 4 of them. Read how Heaton Norris Rovers moved from one ground to another in the 1880s, including a farm, to become Stockport County in 1890 - their first **'gentleman player'** Dr. Blades - very early match reports - first League tables - initial International player Martin John Earp joins in 1900 and dresses in an hotel.

The names of all the early football teams are included plus the **first League Tables** in **Stockport** in the **1890s.** Stockport CC experimented with both rugby and association football around 1890, read how 10,000 people witnessed a **Cheshire Cup Final** staged at **Cale Green** between Crewe Alexandra and Northwich Victoria.

Many of the regions **Golf Clubs** were founded around **1900,** their history is included showing how many started out with a 9 hole golf course, before developing to the 18 they have today. It is interesting to read how much it cost to build a course, and the price of food & drink served at the 19th hole!

**Stockport** has had one of the **most successful Lacrosse clubs in the country**, the unusual start of the team and how the sport became so popular in the late 19th century and beyond.

**Bowls** was another sport which rapidly grew before the end of the century, many clubs were next to public houses and still exist today. Stockport Cricket Club's Bowling Section possessed one of the largest memberships at this time, both at their Hillgate and Cale Green grounds. There were several **Tennis** clubs which were founded alongside bowling teams or cricket clubs.

Finally, there is an **excellent selection of 75 old photographs, covering almost every sport featured in the book, the oldest dating back to 1875.**

The **book covers** the development of **sport** in and around **Stockport** from **early in the 19th century**, through the **Victorian period** and **up to World War 1** - by then, the majority of popular sports were established. In some instances, I have struggled to read photo-copies of photo-copies and other hard to decipher manuscripts, recording a large slice of Stockport history, which could have disappeared forever into the mists of time!

# SPORT AROUND STOCKPORT: THE EARLY YEARS

**B**ritain has a fine tradition of sporting innovation, many of the major sports were started or developed in this country and are now played all over the world!

**Football,** as we know it, evolved in the 19th century from a game played by vast numbers of young men, in the streets or on open land with few or no rules. Starting around 1820, different sets of rules were introduced at each public school or university - making it almost impossible for one to play a match against the other! In 1846, Rugby School published the laws of football as played at their school, rather than containing all the laws of the game.

In 1848, a number of old students from Eton, Harrow, Winchester, Rugby and Shrewsbury met at Cambridge to produce a list of rules. The earliest record of a football club dates back to 1849. Surrey F.C. were founded by members of several cricket clubs, playing a game more rugby based than soccer. The oldest Association Football Club in the World is Sheffield F.C., which started out in 1857 and is still around today! The club produced their own set of rules in October 1858.

The Football Association was founded in 1863 after a series of meetings in London and was really the first split between Soccer and Rugby. There were to be many different versions of the game for years to come, sometimes one half of a match was the 'kicking' game and the second half the 'carrying' method! The next big milestone was the introduction of the F.A. Cup in 1871, the first Finals played at the Oval Cricket Ground. Professionalism was legalised in 1885 and the Football League was established in 1888 with just one Division. There were to be many rule changes for Football, well past the turn of the century.

Until now, the earliest reference to **Cricket** was thought to be in 1597, then called *creckett*. A recent discovery of a 1533 poem attributed to John Skelton, in which he criticised the Flemish weavers who set up home in the South and East of England in the 1300s. He wrote: 'O lorder of Ipocrites, now shut vpp your wickettes, and clape to your clickettes, A! Farewell, kings of crekettes!' The name may have been derived from the Middle Dutch *krick(-e)*, meaning a stick; or the Old English *cricc* or *cryce* meaning a crutch or staff. Another possible source is the Middle Dutch word *krickstoel*, meaning a long low stool, which resembled the long low wicket with 2 stumps used in early cricket.

The first reference to a game is found in a 1597 court case, when a coroner testified that he and his school friends had played *creckett* 50 years earlier - the school was the Royal Grammar School, Guildford. Village cricket had developed by the middle of the 17th century but county cricket had not begun until 1709.

The basic rules of cricket such as bat and ball, the wicket, pitch dimensions, overs, how out, have existed since time immemorial. In 1728, the Duke of Richmond and Alan Brodick drew up 'Articles of Agreement' to determine the code of practice in a particular game. In 1744, the laws of cricket were codified for the first time and then amended in 1774 - when innovations such as lbw, middle stump and maximum bat width were added. The codes were drawn up at the 'Star and Garter Club', whose members ultimately founded the MCC at Lord's in 1787.

All the modern county clubs, starting with Sussex, were founded during the 19th century and in 1864, over arm bowling was legalised. The first ever international game was between the USA and Canada in 1844 - in 1859, a team of leading English professionals set off to North America on the first overseas tour, and in 1862, the first English team toured Australia.

A painting of cricket being played on the Artillery Ground in London, 1743

The exact origins of the sport of **Golf** are unclear - the most widely accepted theory is that it originated in Scotland in the High Middle Ages. The game was mentioned in two 15th century Acts of Parliament, prohibiting the playing of the game of *gowf,* The word *golf* may be a Scots alteration of Dutch '*kolf*' meaning 'stick, club and bat'. The first permanent golf course originated in Scotland, as did membership of the first golf clubs. The very first written rules originated there, as did the establishment of the 18 hole course. The first formalised tournaments developed and competitions were held between various Scottish cities.

Before long, the modern game of golf had spread from Scotland to England and from there to the rest of the world. The oldest playing golf course in the world is The Old Links at Musselburgh Racecourse - evidence has shown that golf was played at Musselburgh Links in 1672, although Mary, Queen of Scots reputedly had a round in 1567!

Golf courses have not always had 18 holes - the original St. Andrews Links, on a narrow strip of land on Queen Mary of Scots estate along the sea, featured 11 holes laid out end to end from the clubhouse. One played the holes out, turned round, and played the holes in for a total of 22 holes. In 1764, several of the holes were deemed too short, and were often combined - the number was thereby reduced from 11 to 9, so that a complete round comprised 18 holes.

**Horse Racing** is one of the most ancient sports and has long been an organised sport in many countries throughout history. Horse racing as a professional sport in the UK, can be traced back to the 12th century after the English knights returned from the Crusades with Arab horses. These horses were bred with English horses to produce the *Thoroughbred Horse* - that is the breed of animal used in horse racing in this country today.

During the reign of Charles 11 from 1660 to 1685, the King held horse races between 2 horses on private courses or open fields with prizes awarded to winners, and Newmarket was the venue for the first horse racing meetings in Britain. Under the reign of Queen Anne during the period 1702-1714, horse races involving several horses, on which spectators placed bets took over from match racing and horse racing became a professional sport with racecourses founded throughout England - Ascot was established by Queen Anne in 1711.

In 1750, horse racing's elite met at Newmarket, to form the Jockey Club to oversee and control English horse racing. This club wrote a comprehensive set of rules for the sport and sanctioned racecourses to conduct horse racing meetings under their rules.

Steps were taken to regulate the breeding of race horses and James Weatherby, an accountant of the Jockey Club, was assigned the task to trace the pedigree and compile the family history of all race horses in England - the result of his work was the introduction to the General Stud Book being published in 1791.

In 1814, races for 3 year olds were designated as 'classics': The 2000 Guineas, the Epsom Derby and the St. Ledger - all open to colts and fillies.

**Tennis** as the modern sport can be dated to two separate roots. Between 1859 and 1865, Major Harry Gem and his friend Augurio Perera developed a game that combined elements of rackets similar to the game of Poona or Badminton - brought by many British soldiers stationed in India and the Basque ball game Pelota. They played on Perera's croquet lawn in Birmingham. In 1872, along with 2 local doctors, they founded the world's first tennis club in Leamington Spa.

In December 1873, Major Clopton Wingfield designed a similar game, which he called *Sphairistike* ('skill at playing at ball') - for the amusement of his guests at a garden party on his estate at Nantclwyd, in Llanelidan, Wales. He based the game on the newer sport of outdoor tennis or real tennis. According to most historians, modern tennis terminology also derives from this period, as Wingfield borrowed both the name and much of the French vocabulary of real tennis and applied them to his new game.

The first championships at Wimbledon were played in 1877. In May 1881, the United States National Lawn Tennis Association was formed to standardise the rules and organise competitions. The U.S. National Men's Singles Championship (U.S. Open) was first held in 1881 at Newport, Rhode Island. The women's Singles Championship followed in 1887. Tennis was also popular in France - their Open dates to 1891.

The start of **Rugby** is traditionally accepted, when a certain William Webb Ellis, first took the ball in his arms and ran with it at Rugby School in 1823. There were various disputes with the rules before the Rugby Football Union was formed at a meeting of 21 clubs in 1871, in the Pall Mall Restaurant, Regent Street and immediately made 'hacking' and 'tripping' illegal! The RFU wanted to standardize the rules and remove some of the more violent aspects of the Rugby School game - this job was completed in June 1871.

There were no rules on amateurism or professionalism until 1886. By 1893 reports of some players in the north of England receiving payments for playing were reaching the RFU on a regular basis! Following a complaint from the Cumberland County Union that another club had lured one of their players away with monetary incentives, the Union established a committee to investigate! The matter came to a head

Brunswick Lacrosse · A Game of Lacrosse · England Tour '83

in 1893 at a meeting at the Westminster Palace Hotel, when a proposal that *'players be allowed compensation for bona fide loss of time'* was outvoted by 282 to 136 votes.

The matter didn't end there and several Yorkshire clubs resigned from the Yorkshire Union and were now Rugby outcasts! At a meeting in Leeds in 1895, 12 clubs agreed they should form a Northern Union and break all links with the Yorkshire Union.

**Bowls** is another equally old pastime. Southampton and Chesterfield believe their bowling greens date back to the 13th century - Hereford claims theirs were laid in 1484. During the 16th and 17th centuries, bowls was the national game - we all know about Sir Francis Drake! Even Kings and labourers, nuns and wives played too! The first reference to a bowling green in Manchester appeared in 1783 near to Strangeways Hall. The first set of modern rules for the game, drafted by a Glasgow solicitor, were in 1849 - a later set was published by George and Thomas Royle, Bowls Makers of Tib Street, Manchester, on behalf of Broughton Cricket Club, in 1868.

**Lacrosse** has its origins in north America, where for centuries tribal teams, often made up of hundreds, played this ancient ball game fast and furiously across great distances. French settlers in the 17th century noted that the strangely formed sticks resembled a bishop's crozier, or 'crosse'. Not until 1867, in Montreal was La Crosse codified for European consumption. That same year, the first of many exhibition tours were undertaken by Canadian teams to venues across the USA, Britain, France and Ireland - resulting in the start of 5 clubs in England. A second more commercial tour by teams of white Canadians and American Indians - the latter playing in war paint and feathers - followed in 1876.

The modern game of **Hockey** grew out of a game which was played in English public schools in the 19th century. Games played with balls and curved sticks can be found throughout history - pictures dating back 4000 years ago have been found in Egypt depicting such events. The first written recording of the word *hockey* can be found in the Galway Statutes of 1527.

The first official club which resembles hockey clubs found today, originated in Blackheath in South East London in 1849. The modern rules developed from those used by members of the Middlesex Cricket Club, who played the game as their winter sport. It has been argued, that the modern form of the sport resembles the style associated with the Teddington (London) Hockey Club - the players introduced the idea of a striking circle, and changed the original rubber cube, used as the ball, into a sphere. The Hockey Association was formed in 1886.

**Billiards** is a game which Mary Queen of Scots loved to play, as did Louis XIV. But in 1757, the Whig government decided that the sport encouraged gambling, and threatened £10 fines for any publicans caught with tables on their premises!

The exact origins of billiards are unclear. Most often credited are the French, who, in the 16th century, transferred a game similar to croquet from outdoors to indoors, and from ground level to a cloth-covered table top. What is certain is that the modern table and its fixtures and fittings were developed by John Thurston, a former apprentice at the Gillow furniture factory in London, who set up on his own in 1799 - he pioneered the slate beds in 1826 under the table's surface to improve the run of the balls.

**Swimming** is Britain's most popular physical recreation after walking. A number of public baths are considered amongst this country's finest examples of 19th and 20th century civic architecture. The Greengate Baths, Collier Street, Salford, dating from 1856, are regarded as this country's first modern baths. Other early public baths are: Blackfriars Street, Salford (1880), Harpurhey, Rochdale Road (1910) and Henry Square Baths, Ashton (1870).

Original Swimming Baths at Cheadle Hulme School, one of the first schools to have this facility c1900

Britain's first **Skating** club is thought to have formed in Edinburgh as early as 1642. In earlier centuries, the big freeze lasted longer when the public used rivers, lakes and ponds i.e. 14 weeks in 1410. In 1819, the Thames at Lambeth froze to a depth of 12 feet from November to March! Members of the Royal Toxopholite (Archery) Society formed a club at Regent's Park in 1830, while out in the Fens, crowds of up to 10,000 gathered along ice-bound canals to bet on speed skating races between farm labourers. The first attempt to make a substitute for ice in Baker Street, London in 1841, offered skaters a surface of crystallised alum, hog's lard, soda salt and melted sulphur. It felt like hardened cheese, smelt awful, and falling over on it was not recommended!

The game of **Croquet** can be traced back to the middle ages to a pastime called 'Pall Mall', played in London and from which the well-known street is named. This involved hitting a single ball through very wide hoops. The origins of the modern game are reputed to have started in Ireland in the 1830s and taken to England during the 1850s. It became an instant success - the first opportunity for women to participate in an outdoor sport on an equal basis with men! The first national headquarters was the Wimbledon All England Croquet Club, founded in 1868, which later was to become the Wimbledon All England Tennis & Croquet Club. Tennis overshadowed the sport and towards the turn of the century, croquet was in decline - it is no accident that the size of a tennis court is exactly half that of a croquet lawn!

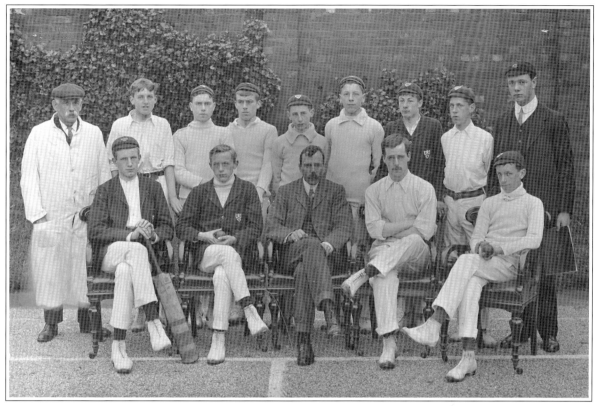

Stockport Grammar School Cricket team in 1910

**Stockport Grammar School** was founded in **1487**, by Sir Edmund Shaa, Alderman and then Mayor of London in 1482. Shortly before he died, he made a will, which included funds to establish a grammar school in his native Stockport - the initial site was St. Mary's Church, in the centre of the old town. Later there were moves to Chestergate and the corner of what is now Wellington Road South and Greek Street (1832), before the present location at Mile End in 1916.

In 1837 and 1839, land was purchased for play grounds, which was further extended in 1853. A field in the area must have been rented for sport, because the first cricket match was played in September 1860:

> *'STOCKPORT GRAMMAR SCHOOL v. ST. PETER'S GRAMMAR SCHOOL\* - These Elevens met on Wednesday last to play a match (we believe the "maiden" of both Clubs), which after a spirited contest ended in favour of the former, with 8 wickets to spare. The 'batting' was pretty good on both sides; but it was evident that the St. Peter's eleven were nowhere in fielding (with one honourable exception, Master T. Hudson). The Stockport Grammar School Eleven, on the contrary, fielded admirably. We understand the return match is to be played at an early day, and we doubt not it will be a well-contested one on both sides. We subjoin the scores:- GRAMMAR AND FREE SCHOOL 73 and 4 for 2, ST. PETER'S GRAMMAR SCHOOL 42 AND 31'.*

\*Levenshulme

The first evidence of rugby being played came in 1874, when the School 2nd team of 15 players (2 goals, 1 poster, 6 touchdowns, 5 rouges) were against Crusaders, who fielded 17 players (1 rouge).

In 1902, advice on drill was introduced from a Captain Bradshaw 'to improve the bearing and physical condition of the boys'. Fifty pupils had joined the school Cricket Club, practising regularly on the Stockport Cricket Club ground. In 1907, the Old Boys Association had raised £1,600, to buy a 4 acre playing field in Adswood and Old Boy T.C. Norris, donated £500 for cricket equipment. A small pavilion was erected and a groundsman employed at £1 4s. a week, plus a stable built (£14) and horse (£3) for pulling the roller. These playing fields were officially opened in 1910. The school 'Year Book' for this year listed sports as follows:

### The School Cricket Club

Mr. Green is the Honorary Secretary and superintends the extra cricket practice on whole School Days. The different elevens have interesting lists of fixtures with various Schools within reach. Mr. Green and Mr. Adams coach the boys and in this work receive valuable help from Sam Brown, the School Professional.

### The School Football Club

Mr. Green is the Honorary Secretary: he arranges matches with suitable opponents and practice matches are frequently played on the School Ground. Mr. Adams and Mr. Scutt have rendered great help in the coaching and 'refereeing.'

### The School Lacrosse Club
Mr. South is the Secretary of the Lacrosse Club —- this game has only been played in the School for a short time, but a good standard of play has been reached, and the various elevens have met with with considerable success in their matches. Mr. Smith and Mr. Helm have been of great assistance in coaching the boys.

### School Athletic Sports
These Sports are held annually in the School Ground. Medals are given to the winners and to those who reach the 'Standard' in the various events. The School Championship Cup and the Junior Championship Cup are awarded on the results of certain events in the Sports. Mr. Green is the Honorary Secretary of the Sports.

Another Old Boy, George Norris, gave a sum of £1,000 to build a Gymnasium, dedicated to his, and his brother's memory in 1913.

The **first** documentary evidence of any **sport in the area** dates back to **1764,** with details about **Stockport Races.** The Races took place on Great Moor, with the horses starting the race in a field where Cherry Tree Hospital now stands - not surprisingly known as the 'Starting in Field'. There were instructions for entrants to the event, to join the course at Jepson's Barn, near to the distance post. The horse racing took place from Tuesday 10th - 12th July that year.

The initial race on the card was for a prize of £50, a considerable sum of money in 1764! It was open to any horse at least 4 years old, which had never won this value prize money in the past, carrying a weight of 8 stone - the best of 3 x 2 mile heats.

On the Wednesday, £50 prize again for horses 14 hands, to carry 9 st. - the best of 3 x 4 mile races. Thursday for same prize money, for 5 and 6 year olds. Horses 5 years to carry 8st. 7lbs. and 6 years to take 9st. 8lbs. - 3 x 4 mile heats.

Regular subscribers to the races paid 1 guinea (£1 5p) entrance fee and non subscribers 3 guineas plus 10s 6d. to the clerk of the course for weights, scales etc. No less that 3 reputed horses had to start any of the races - if only 2 horses enter, entrance money was returned. All the above plates were subject to the Kings Plate Articles and paid without deduction - Stewards: Sir George Warren and John Chetwode Esq.

The Stockport Races were an annual event and were sanctioned by the nobility and principal gentry of the county. 'The balls in the evening were of the most elegant and fashionable description'. It is unknown exactly when the races on Great Moor ceased to exist, but no mention of them after 1822.

The first Sunday Schools were established in Stockport in 1784. **Stockport Sunday School** was founded in **1794 -** many years later, the founder members of Stockport County were to be educated here. The first stone for the new building, high above Wellington Street (now demolished) was laid on 15th June 1805. The estimated cost for the largest Sunday School in the country was £4000, to accommodate 4,000 children.

'The cost of the education for one poor child's education was £1 - the annual expenditure of 1s (5p) per annum for each child. The majority of the children were from the labouring classes. Essentially a Conservative institution, providing religious teaching and instruction in reading and writing for young people and improving leisure activities which served to promote respectable working-class attitudes'.

There were various exercises outlined for the children every Sunday in reading and writing. The other early Sunday Schools in the area were: Brinksway, Lancashire Hill, Heaviley and Heaton Mersey.

The first sports to be introduced were cricket, football and athletics. The ground used for many years for such sports was at Edgeley Fold, off Edgeley Road (now Alexandra Park). In the 1902-03 football season, the team reached the semi-final of the Stockport & District Cup v Poynton. The match was played at Stockport County's old ground, Green Lane - the game didn't start until 4pm, Poynton winning by 4-0. The football team, played in the 1st Division of the Stockport & District League.

Other sports to follow were: Tennis, Hockey, Lacrosse, Cycling and Bowling. Facilities were established at Nangreave Road in 1927 - this land was given by the Ward family from the hatting industry.

The oldest newspaper for the town, was the *Stockport Advertiser,* printed and published by James Lomas in Great Underbank, first introduced in April, 1822. The only mention of Sporting activities in that first issue were of a forthcoming National Boxing Championship bout, Crib v Neale, Trotting (horses) matches in Surrey and past news about horse breeding! Not surprising, when you consider there was as yet no organised football, rugby or tennis and cricket, bowls and golf were still in their infancy!

There was then, little in the way of sport in Stockport, but included were other items from across the country, particularly horse racing. What would now be looked upon as barbaric pastimes, people were betting on: Dog fighting, how long it would take a dog to kill 100 rats and Cock fighting!

Horse Racing as it would have looked at the time of Stockport Races

**Cheadle** was another village which possessed a **Horse Racing Course,** sited next to Manchester Road - it was considered important enough to be listed along with the other main Race-courses of the country. The first mention of Cheadle Races was in September **1823**; 'Several valuable cups and other prizes will be run for, and great anxiety prevails amongst the sporting characters in this neighbourhood as to the entry, which we have heard will exceed that of any former year'.

Earlier, in September 1836, the meeting attracted a crowd from neighbouring towns of 10,000 - even though the weather was poor. There would be attractions for the whole family, resulting in a big day out. Horse Racing was one of the few outdoor sports to attract the masses.

In September 1845, there was a 3 day meeting from Monday to Wednesday. The first event being 'sweepstake for 3 sovereign's with 20 added' - Mr. Lamb's 'Lady Flora' declared the winner. The Stockport Stakes for '2 Sovs. each 10 added' - won by Mr. Mason's 'Lucy'. Tuesday consisted of the Manchester Stakes (2 Sovs.), Ladies Purse (1 Sov.) and the New Stakes Sweepstake (1 Sov.) To finish on Wednesday, were the Cheadle Stakes (2 Sovs.) and

Sweepstakes (1 Sovs.) The large sum of £100 prize money was offered in the grand finale race - won by Mr. Brown's 'Chum'.

In **1830** Stockport Harriers were meeting in Poynton and completed 4 runs of considerable duration - 'members of the hunt horses, being more than usually swift, the gallant pack killed twice!'

There is reference to Horse Racing taking place in what were called the 'Back Fields', opposite the 'Ash Inn', Manchester Road in 1830. Also taking place in the then nearby canal, was 'Duck Swimming'. A duck was put in the water and a number of dogs were let loose to catch it - the owner of the successful dog claimed the duck!

'At Hatherlow (near Romiley), there was a Pigeon Match for £5 a side between 2 crack shots. However, when 5 birds each had been shot, a dispute arose and it was brought to a wrangle. Mr. Marlow of Newton (near Hyde) and Mr. Ford of Stockport. Marlow's 5th bird was shot 20 yards outside the boundary at the 'Hare & Hounds'. The contest did not proceed further!

Quite clearly, in the 19th century, betting on any kind of sport, was as popular then as it is today.

The nearest equivalent to today's marathon was staged in 1830 for the sum of £20, between a Mr. C. Crossley, a tin plate worker of Stockport and Thomas Hudson, a butcher of Cheadle. The course was from the 'Wellington Inn', Heaviley to Horwich End beyond Whaley Bridge and back in the quickest time - Crossley was to be given a 2 miles start. The whole distance for the butcher was 20 miles - **'Hudson a far more likely man of youth and strength than Crossley, 15 years older. Crossley finished the end of the race before him in 3 hours 34 minutes, both men dreadfully distressed and put to bed immediately on their coming in, and though the butcher was so beaten as to fall down in a state of insensibility when within sight of Crossley, the opinion of everyone who saw the race, had it not been for the injudicious treatment of the young man, during the race, by his backers and friends who supplied him with stimulants until drunk, he must certainly have won the race. Much interest and thousands of people'**

**Horse Racing** was taking place in **Bullock Smithy** (Hazel Grove). The site of the horse racing was behind the 'Rising Sun' alongside what is now Macclesfield Road - there would not have been any stands, just an open field. Due to the tradition of the races, the racecourse estate off Torkington Road was so named.

One meeting started on Tuesday August 10th **1830** for 3 days duration. 'The subscription purse of 50 pence with 10 pence added, was won by Mr. Marlow's 'Chance', beating Mr. Prescott's 'Moss Rose' and Mr. Wragg's 'Fanny My Dear'. The Pony Race was won by Mr. Pott's, beating Boldworth's pony and another'.

On Wednesday, there was the Ladies' Plate, won by Mr. Arthur's bay mare, beating Mr. Marlow's 'Chance', Mr. Weatherall's 'Footman' and Mr. Pott's bay mare.

Thursday saw the Landlords' Purse race - won by Mr. Pott's 'Little Bo Peep', beating Mr. Arthur's bay filly, Mr. Pott's 'Feather Weight', Mr. Wragg's 'Fanny My Dear' and Mr. Weatherall's 'Footman'.

A well known venue for Cock Fighting was the 'Grapes Inn', which closed in 1845. For one year, Badger-baiting took place in a yard adjoining the Inn. The badger, a ferocious animal, was placed in a long wooden trough, dogs were let loose upon it one at a time. The dog drawing the badger out won the prize - a cruel sport for both animals!

There was a Foot Race in 1831, between 2 'Journeymen Hatters' aged 47 and 67. 'The younger man gave the older one a quarter mile, they started at the Chapel House and ran the Manchester and Buxton Road towards Stockport - the older won the wager easily, his opponent performed the mile in little less than 6 minutes'.

Stockport Hounds met at Poynton, the same year, a £50 bet was on with a Stalybridge rider - who could jump the highest leap!

In 1832, like many towns in the country, Bull-baiting was taking place. One location was in a field behind an unamed beerhouse in Green Lane, Heaton Norris - more than likely the 'Nursery Inn', where Stockport County were to play years later.

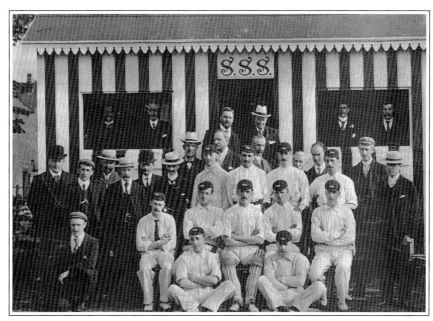

The opening of Stockport Sunday School's new pavilion in 1903 at Edgeley Fold, Edgeley Road

**The first report of a Cricket Match in Stockport was in July 1836.** The match was between 2 elevens from the Stockport Trades Club, played at the Churchgate

Ground (Rectory Fields), now covered by new houses but retaining the original name, the scores: 'Blues'* 65 and 32, 'Scarlets'* 62 and 76 - *colour of their caps. Cricket, in these early years, would still be featuring under arm bowling - over arm would not be legalised until 1864. Prior to this date, there will have been a combination of the two, but it would have to have been agreed between the 2 captains before the start of a match.

Another game to feature this year, was in August, when the Stockport Club were up against the Trades Club, played at the former, the scores: Stockport 95 and 100, Trades 64 & 37.

The early cricket clubs in Stockport of any importance, were known respectively as 'The Gentlemen's Club' and 'The Stockport Tradesmen's Club'. In later years, in both cricket and football, we found 'Gentlemen' and 'Players' in the same team, but going back even further we have 2 clubs in place to separate social standing!

The Gentlemen's Club played in a field on the Heaton Mersey Road, opposite to the 'Club House Inn', Heaton Norris. Messrs John Eskrigge, W.L. Eskrigge, Robert Holt, W. Sykes, James Barratt, and S.R. Wilkinson were prominent members. This club was dissolved in 1849, owing to a scarcity of players. After payment was made for the expense of a dinner for the members, there remained a balance of £3 5s. (£3.25) - this sum was handed over to the treasurer of the Stockport Infirmary, to be applied to the benevolent subjects of that Institution.

The 'Club House' Inn, Travis Brow, Stockport Gentleman's Cricket Club played opposite the Inn

The Tradesmen's Club initially played in a field owned by a Mr. Farrant at Churchgate, before moving to Heaton Norris, in a field off George's Road, then familiarly known as 'Donkey Park' and later forming the site of the Railway Goods Station of the Cheshire Lines Committee. Amongst the playing members of this club were Richard Selby, David Williamson, George Fogg, and John Clarke.

On the breaking up of the Gentlemen's Club, the Tradesmen's Club moved to the ground near to the 'Club House' and then in 1850 to a field at Cheadle Heath, opposite to the 'Farmers Arms'. A short time afterwards, this club changed grounds again, to a field off Wellington Road South, between Spring Bank Mill and Stockport Railway Station. In 1853, the Tradesmen's Club folded, and briefly, little interest seems to have been taken in cricket in Stockport.

Poynton Park was the out of town venue in 1837, for a cricket match between 11 players of the Stockport Trades Club v 10 players from the Stockport Junior outfit (late Churchgate Club). The Trades were favourites at 6 to 4 even, but at the end of the 1st innings, betting had changed to 3 & 4 to 1. The scores: Stockport Trades 33 and 26, Stockport Junior 69. 'Numerous spectators had assembled to witness this manly game'.

Below is a report of a cricket game in August, 1838, played at Churchgate:

*'The return cricket match between the Victoria and the Stockport Clubs was played on Wednesday last, in a field in Churchgate, by permission of Mr. Farrant. The weather continued showery during the match, which prevented many from witnessing the game. After a well played game, the Victoria party defeated their opponents in one innings with three notches to spare. Emlow and Wilkinson proved themselves the best players in the field. Emlow bowled 14 wickets down out of the 20, and obtained eight notches, whilst Wilkinson scored 11, and fielded admirably'.*

For the record, Stockport scored 15 and 23 to the Victoria Clubs' 41. This match was very low scoring even by the standards of the 1830's, but when you consider the 'basic' state of the wickets then, and the 'dubious' quality of the bats - not really surprising!

The **All England Bowling Stakes** were held in **1839** at the 'White Hart', Cheadle by kind permission of Mr. Parkinson. There were 16 bowlers on each side - the Stakes were won by Mr. Butcher of Chowbent v Mr. Nuttall of Bolton, betting was even at the start, before a crowd of 500 people. 'Sixty of Mr. Parkinson's sporting friends sat down to an excellent dinner and bowled tots of old crusted port over the tongue'! One of the party from Bolton was open to bowl any man in England, each to bowl with his feet, for any sum from £10 to £100.

The small column in the *Stockport Advertiser*, which featured sports, went under the heading of 'Sporting Intelligence'. It often showed more national than local sports news, one of which could be described as the **first International Cricket match** in **1840**:

FRANCE v ENGLAND
*'On Monday and Tuesday week a grand match of Cricket was played at the sweet little village of River, near Dover, between 11 cricketers from Calais and 11 in the neighbourhood, when the men of River, after an admirably contested field, were triumphant, they having 7 wickets to go down. The return match is to be played at Calais Downs shortly. Much interest was excited by the match and not fewer than 3,000 persons were on the ground the first day'.*

It is surprising that there was any cricket being played in France at this time - I don't think this game has been classified as a Test Match!

**Wilmslow Races** were in evidence in **1841**, located at Lindow Common - now the site of Racecourse Road. A 2 day event in August, on a Tuesday, Ladies Purse for 6 sovereigns & Wilmslow Stake and Wednesday included among others, the Railway Stake.
There was a report of a forthcoming Foot Race in 1842 between William Brown of Stockport v Samuel Aspinall of Reddish. 'They had been matched to run 150 yards for £12 a side - to come off on Easter Monday at the Snipe Inn, Ashton-under-Lyne. Aspinall is training at Reddish and Brown at the Traveller's Call, Bredbury. The former is favourite at present'.

**Foot Race Ground** - 'We understand that Mr.Kirk of the Traveller's Call Bredbury is finishing at his own expense, a convenient foot race ground 200 yards in length, through some fields in his occupation. It will be a great accommodation to the pedestrians of the neighbourhood'.

There was always a listing in the local newspaper of the Hunting Fixtures of the Cheshire Fox Hounds - for instance, in 1843, they met as regularly as November 20, 22, 23, 25, 27, 29, 30 and December 2nd. No doubt the 'gentry' had plenty of time on their hands - the closest they came to Stockport was Alderley Park.

In **1844** there was a 3 day programme at **Heaviley Races** starting on Monday September 16th. The opening day started with the Trial Stakes for 5 Sovereigns (£5) each plus a silver plated mounted whip, value 2 guineas - won by Mr. Cronshaw's 'Fanny'. Next came a Plate for 7 Sovs., and finally The Cup Sweepstakes. Tuesday started with the Borough Cup and then the Sweepstakes at 5 Sovs. each. Wednesday had the Plate at 5 Sovs. Each and a Cup valued at £5. 'Too much praise cannot be given to Mr. George Crook, Veterinary Surgeon for his exertions as clerk of the course, the best order having been maintained throughout the meeting'.

In July, 1844 there was a cricket match of great interest in Stockport, Cotton Manufacturers v Other Trades & Professions. I quote below the full match report - cricket lovers will not have seen a scorecard quite like this one:

CRICKET
*'On Monday last, two-and-twenty members of our respectable and rising cricket club, had a trial of their capabilities at their excellent ground near the Club House, Heaton Norris. An arrangement had been made for eleven manufacturers to play eleven other gentlemen engaged in other trades and professions, all members of the club; and on the fine and favourable afternoon of Monday, this interesting match was decided.*
*It will be seen from the subjoined score that the manufacturers were very easy winners; but had their opponents only met with the usual run of casualties, the match would have been better and more evenly contested.*
*In both innings the 'professions and trades' were exceedingly unfortunate in losing Mr. Cholmondeley (from whom they anticipated great assistance) without making a single run; and in their last innings, one or two of their 'crack' players were bowled out without scoring a single notch. The batting and bowling of Messrs Barratt, Howard, and Holt, on one side, were admirable, whilst the fielding of Messrs Billingham, Swires, and Brown was no less accomplished on the other.*
*The great improvement which has taken place in the play of every member of this promising club is quite evident, and we have not the slightest doubt, but that in any match in which it may be presently be engaged, it will be found a very dangerous and formidable opponent'*

## COTTON MANUFACTURERS

| First Innings | | | Second Innings | |
|---|---|---|---|---|
| Barrat, bowled out by J. Nash | 26 | —— | Caught by Walker | 14 |
| Howard, b out by ditto | 8 | —— | b out by Brown | 9 |
| Holt, b out by ditto | 41 | —— | c by Cholmondeley | 21 |
| S. Wilkinson b out by ditto | 0 | —— | b out by J. Nash | 1 |
| Roberts, caught by E. Nash | 1 | —— | c by ditto | 1 |
| J. Robinson, b out by Billingham | 2 | —— | b out by Brown | 0 |
| H. Robinson, b out by ditto | 0 | —— | c by Swires | 1 |
| S.H. Cheetham, c by Smith | 8 | —— | c by E. Nash | 2 |
| J. Cheetham, not out | 1 | —— | c by Brown | 1 |
| T. Brooke, b out by Pearce | 0 | —— | not out | 0 |
| Axon, run out | 0 | —— | b out by Brown | 0 |
| **Byes, & c** | **3** | —— | **Byes, & c** | **2** |
| | **90** | | | **62** |

## OTHER TRADES AND PROFESSIONS

| First Innings | | | Second Innings | |
|---|---|---|---|---|
| Billingham, b out by Barrat | 6 | —— | c by S.H. Cheetham | 4 |
| J. Nash, b out by Howard | 2 | —— | c by ditto | 1 |
| Brown, b out by Barratt | 19 | —— | b out by Barratt | 0 |
| Pearce, b out by ditto | 5 | —— | b out by Howard | 6 |
| E. Nash, b out by ditto | 13 | —— | Run out | 9 |
| Smith, b out by ditto | 0 | —— | b out by Howard | 7 |
| Cholmondeley, leg before wicket | 0 | —— | b out by Holt | 0 |
| Swires, not out | 9 | —— | b out by Howard | 7 |
| Vaughan, b out by Barratt | 0 | —— | c by Barratt | 0 |
| Harrop, b out by ditto | 0 | —— | not out | 5 |
| Walker, c by S.H. Cheetham | 0 | —— | c by Holt | 8 |
| **Byes, & c** | **11** | —— | **Byes** | **3** |
| | **65** | | | **50** |

It is interesting to note, that when a player was out caught, the bowler was not credited with the wicket. Even though all the participants were members of a gentleman's club, there were only a few who 'qualified' to have initials before their name!

In July 1845, the Stockport CC had a fixture v the Broughton Club (one of the oldest clubs in Manchester), played at Stockport. Scores as follows:

**Broughton 1st Innings 54 (19 overs) - 2nd Innings 42 (16 overs)**
**Stockport 1st Innings 49 (19 overs) - 2nd Innings 42 (13 overs)**
**Broughton won by 7 notches - W. Moss (Broughton) was the only player on either side to reach double figures!**

Another fixture that summer for Stockport was v Manchester Victoria, a return match played at Manchester. Wickets were 'pitched' at 10am, the game starting at 11am - Stockport scored 114 from 51 overs and the Manchester team made 92 from 33 overs. As early as 1845, there were professional cricketers - 'Stockport's Mr. Cornell was not available, as engaged to play in the Norfolk match the following day (Tuesday)'.

In the same month and year, Stockport Cricket Club played a match v Knutsford, staged on Knutsford Race-Course. The scores were: Knutsford 42 and 94, Stockport 67 and 71 - 'Total Stockport 138 with 4 wickets to spare Knutsford 136'.

There was a match between the Stockport Cricket Club and 8 'Gentlemen' of the town of Stockport + 2 from the Manchester Broughton Club and Mr. Selby of the Stockport Club, 'given' to the 'Gentlemen's' team. The encounter took place on the 10th and 17th

July, 1852 - a week's gap to finish the game! The 2 Manchester 'Gentlemen' were 'absent' for the 2nd innings, which gave the Stockport Club a great advantage - winning by 6 wickets.

**Stockport Cricket Club** was founded back in **1855** and originally named the Cale Green Club. The members of this new club consisted mainly of employees of Messrs. S. & T. Carrington, of the Cale Green Hat Works - the company providing the materials necessary to start the club. The cricket ground was a field adjoining the present ground at Adswood Lane, and was rented from Mr. C.R. Brady. Messrs W.H. Brady, C.A. Brady, J. Staveacre, J.O. Williams and J. Fleming who were among the most active originators of the club. The Cale Green Club attracted the best players in the town, and soon began to be called Stockport Cricket Club.

Still in existence, displayed in a glass case at Cale Green, is the very **first set of rules** laid down by the committee which now makes interesting reading:

1. That the club be called 'The Stockport Cricket Club'.
2. That it is managed by a President, two Vice Presidents, a Secretary, a Treasurer, with a Committee of twelve of the members, five of whom form a quorum.*
3. That the Secretary be the Executive of the Committee, in all cases when he may consider a committee meeting unnecessary.
4. That an Annual General Meeting of the club be called in January, for the election of Officers, auditing the accounts and transacting general business.
5. That new members be elected either at a

A rare example of an early cricket match at Cheadle Hulme School

committee meeting or at the general meeting.

6. That the annual subscription be 10/6d., due on demand after the first of March.
7. That Honorary members be admitted at a voluntary subscription of not less than 10s 6d.
8. That Honorary members, paying an annual subscription of 21s., have free admission for themselves and lady friends to all matches, and the privilege of introducing any non-resident friend to practice on the ground.
9. That Naval and Military Officers quartered in Stockport be considered Honorary Members.
10. That the club adopt the laws of cricket of the Marylebone Cricket Club.
11. That Wednesdays and Saturdays be Field Days.
12. That the members appointed to play in a match appear in the recognised costume of the club, viz, white flannel trousers and shirt and blue cap.
13. That the eleven elect their Captain at the commencement of the game, and regard obedience to him throughout it.
14. That the Secretary forward to every new member a list of rules.

*number that must be present to constitute valid meeting*

Whilst the start date for the club is 1855, the first matches were not played until May 1857. A combination of shortage of opponents and a 'fun' match in June that year, there was a match between 11 First X1 'married' players v 22 'single' players from the 2nd and 3rd teams:

*CALE GREEN CRICKET CLUB*
*ELEVEN "MARRIED" v TWENTY TWO*
*"SINGLE"*

*'A very interesting and well-contested Match came off on the above ground on Saturday afternoon last, between the First Eleven "Married," and the Second and Third-Eleven "Single", of the above Club.*
*The weather was particularly propitious; and although this club has been in being some five or six weeks, and consequently scarcely known to the lovers of this fine game; yet we noticed a very large and respectable company of spectators, including a very moderate sprinkling of the fair sex. After the usual tossing for the first innings, two of the Single, Mr. G. Griffith and Mr. C. Atkinson took, their bats, and commenced the game as under, - the first Eleven taking up their positions in the field. In justice to the second and third Elevens, we feel it our duty to state that the first Eleven included the three names well known to the players of this beautiful game, - Messrs. Williamson, Selby, and Fogg.*
*The first inning being ended with a score of 50, the second and third Elevens took up their positions in*

*the field, with one fielder short, - and considering that a great number of these had not played before this season, the fielding was very praiseworthy. Unfortunately, for the Single, in their second fielding, through circumstances unavoidable, they were five fielders short, or, perhaps, the result of the game might have been changed.'*

For the record, the scores were: Married 32 and 58 for 7, Single 50 and 39.

In July, of the 1859 summer, there was a game arranged for Cale Green v the strong Manchester Gentlemen's Club. The Stockport team consisted of 9 of their members plus 2 gentlemen 'drafted in' from Broughton. The revenue raised (£20) was in aid of funds for the Ragged School. Among the visitors were many elegantly dressed ladies and members of the most influential families in the borough. Mr. Higham's Brass Band was provided by the Manchester players at no cost! Seventy players and friends returned to the 'Wellington Inn' to dine after the game, which ended: Cale Green 121, Manchester 65.

I list below examples of some of the other matches played in 1859:

**Cale Green: 38 & 68 for 6 v Newton Heath (Royal Victoria): 45 & 55**
*(Proceeds of the tickets to funds for the Infirmary - boosted the crowd)*
**Cale Green: 56 v Cheetham: 56**
**Cale Green: 71 & 64 v Medical Students: 48 & 59 for 4** *(abandoned due to heavy rain)*
**Stockport: 59 v Haughton Green: 49**
**(THE FIRST MATCH CLUB CALLED STOCKPORT - IN SEPTEMBER)**
**Stockport: 56 v Haughton Green: 15**
**Stockport: 113 v 22 Players of various clubs of the town (Stockport) : 66**

In the early years of Stockport CC, all members were issued with a membership book, which listed the season's fixtures, the club's officers and other information such as bowling matches and club events. The most important use of this book, however, was to allow free admission to the ground. Non-members were not allowed in or in front of the pavilion. These books were small but often had ornate gold leaf decoration, showing that membership of the club was very exclusive! There were often at least 650 members most seasons.

In June 1860, Stockport travelled to Prestbury Road, to play Macclesfield. The Silk Town club, then, called themselves Macclesfield Olympic - a team that considered themselves one of the best in Cheshire! In a very closely fought match, Stockport were the victors by just 8 runs: **Macclesfield 72 & 50, Stockport 39 & 75.** The return game at the end of September, at Stockport, resulted in large win for the home team by an innings and 12 runs: **Stockport 101, Macclesfield 48 & 41.** These 2 results show just how far the Stockport club had developed in just 5 years!

The Macclesfield Olympic Club had the honour of staging a prestige game the same year - Macclesfield & District v an All England X1. The home team added 2 professional bowlers into their side of 22 players, scores: Macclesfield 103 for 10 wickets, England 87.

Stockport Cricket Club held an annual match for several seasons v the County of Chester Club, who were based at Chelford CC. Stockport had big problems raising a team in the 1861 encounter - some of the players did not bother to state they were unavailable! Following a delay of some hours, 8 players from Stockport plus 3 local men were 'rounded up'. Not surprisingly, they lost by 70 runs.

Another prestige game of the period was v the Manchester Club, which played had at Old Trafford from 1857 until the club was developed into Lancashire County CC in 1864. The Manchester team included players brought in from Broughton and Longsight clubs to form a strong outfit. Stockport scored 77 against Manchester's 169.

In 1862, the club left Cale Green, having leased a field at Bramhall Lane, near to the Davenport Railway Station, and here Stockport remained until 1871.

Between 1859 and 1871, Messrs. G.A. Fernley, A.H. Sykes, R. Sykes, J. M'Cance, W.R. Sidebottom, T. Burrows, J. Whatmough, R. Selby, James Needham, F.F. Kelly, J. Galbraith, G. Fogg and J.H. Carrington were well-known players.

By 1870, local cricket was in a very unsatisfactory state - many of the old players had retired or took little interest in the club. The ground at Bramhall Lane was inconvenient, situated some distance from Stockport centre and not easily accessible for practice, which reduced attendances on match days.

Local cricketing talent was divided amongst a number of small clubs, of which the Cheadle Moseley and the Charlestown (their ground was on Bramhall Lane, near to where Stockport Georgians now play) clubs were the best known. These 2 teams, being energetically managed, and possessing many promising players, provided formidable rivals to the Stockport club. Fully realising the danger, which was then imminent, of the cricketing talent and interest in the town being split amongst several clubs, instead of being concentrated in one, they left no stone unturned to persuade leading members of the rival teams to join the Stockport club, and at the same time held out every inducement for an amalgamation with the Premier club.

Mr. Thomas Burrows took a very active part furthering this scheme - his services were most valuable on account of his great personal influence with Stockport cricketers. The end result was that the Cheadle Moseley and Charlestown clubs gradually died out, and most of the members joined the Stockport club, which then became really the representative club of the town.

The following gentlemen, amongst others, came from the 2 clubs, O. Coppock, T.P. Torkington, W. McLachlan (one of the best players Stockport had in this period), H. Torkington, R. Mac.Lachlane, J. Long, T.L. Sutton and J.D. Oakes.

Upon the expiry of the lease of the Bramhall Lane ground in 1870, it was decided to move to a more suitable locality, and accordingly the club leased from Mr. Charles Marsland, a plot of land near Higher Hillgate, which had been used for some time as a running ground in connection with the 'Bowling Green Inn'. The land was later covered by buildings, and intersected by Charles Street, Adcroft Street, Ward Street and Harrop Street. The Inn stood just outside the gates to the ground on what is now Charles Street.

It was not unusual in Victorian times, that public houses held sporting events close to their premises - a good way of increasing revenue! The new ground was laid and prepared by Mr. J.H. Carrington in 1870 for £140 - it is hard to imagine now, that this cricket pitch was later to stage matches v Australia!

The Higher Hillgate Ground was opened on the 13th May 1871, when a match, Stockport v Manchester, was played:

*OPENING CRICKET MATCH*

*'On Saturday last the new ground of Stockport Cricket Club was opened to the public. It is a very eligible site for the purpose, being situate in Higher Hillgate within five minutes walk of the Heaviley road, along which the Hazel Grove omnibuses pass, and within ten minutes' walk of Edgeley Station. It is surrounded on all sides by boarding about 10 feet in height, and we believe the dimensions to be 140 by 130 yards. The pavilion commands a fine view of the Derbyshire hills, and the ground is altogether a very attractive one. Possessing the natural advantages which it does, we shall be surprised if the public of Stockport do not often avail themselves of the new cricket ground as a Saturday's promenade.*

*The attraction held out on Saturday last was a match between the local eleven and an eleven of the Manchester club. In spite of the inclemency of the weather the attendance of visitors was considerable. The band of the Earl of Chester's Yeomanry Cavalry was present and played with their usual efficiency. The bowling and fielding of the*

# Stockport Cricket Club at Hillgate

'Gentlemen' Bowling members in 1875 with pavilion in background. 1 - Jackson, 2 - Whittaker, 3 - Flanagan, 4 - Sutton, 5 - J. Hamlett (Christy Hats), 6 - C. Shore, 7 - J. Hallowell, 8 - Torkington, 9 - T. Sutton (founder Sutton & Torkington Hats) , 10 - J. Calvert, 11 - Norbury (Christy), 12 - Bancroft, 13 - J. Hall, 14 - B. Fletcher ('Blossoms Hotel'), 15 - N. Wild (Christy), 16 - J. Marshall, 17 - J. Horner (Sec. Stockport CC), 18 - T. Smale, 19 - J. Turner, 20 - T. Torkington (founder Sutton & Torkington Hats), 21 - D. Hogg, 22 - J. Selby, 23 - J. Burrows, 24 - G. Atherton (Mayor 1896-7 & 1903), 25 - T. Thorpe, 26 - W. Brown, 27 - J. Davenport, 28 - T. Leah (Stockport SS), 29 - Torkington, 30 - J. Bennett, 31 - W. Wilson, 32 - J. Burrows, 33 - Unknown

*Stockport eleven were capitol, but their batting was unable to cope with the splendid bowling of Hicton, who is without doubt one of the finest professional bowlers in England. The batting of Mr. W. Taylor in the first innings, and Mr. F.L. Thompson in the second, are, however, honourable exceptions, as both these gentlemen batted exceedingly well. The wicket-keeping of Mr. Smith is particularly worthy of notice. On the Manchester side the batting of Messrs Swire, Craig, Hickton, and Allison was good, but Mr. Ollivant decidedly carried off the palm, his innings being a treat which no cricketer could fail to enjoy. Below we give the score:-'*
*Manchester 123, Stockport 42 and 33.*

A report in another newspaper read: 'Hickton's playing was about perfection itself, and his management of the willow was only excelled by his admirable bowling - swift and powerful - *which in many instances was fatal to the middle wicket only'.*

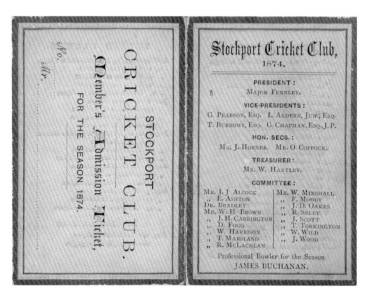

Admission Ticket 1874

At this time, although there was a decided improvement in the club's playing talent, its financial position was anything but satisfactory - in fact amounting to insolvency! After a hard struggle, the committee succeeded in putting the club back on its feet again - making it one of the most popular and influential institutions of the town!

To increase the income of the club, and having noticed that Athletic Sports held in the area proved successful, the committee decided to try one as an experiment. The first sports event took place on the 17th August 1872, and fully realised their expectations - they were held annually up to 1881 and revived again in 1888 for years to come. In 1873, the liabilities of Stockport CC were cleared, resulting out of the profit from the sports days - in celebration of this event, a piece of plate was presented to Mr. William Hartley, the then Secretary, at the annual dinner. Some members objected to the athletics, but the first 16 events made a profit of £1,138 18s. 4d.

A bowling green had been laid at the new Hillgate Ground and the first match was played in September, 1872 v Reddish. The scores: **Doubles - Reddish 65, Stockport 71, Singles - Reddish 93, Stockport 116.**

The oldest surviving Stockport Cricket Club Membership Card, dates back to the 1874 season. It was a few years away before footballers were paid, but cricket had its professionals in place by now - the Professional Bowler for the season was James Buchanan. The fixtures for that summer were:

### FIRST ELEVEN

April 25 - *Opening Day* - Married v. Single
May 2     - ATHLETIC SPORTS
"    " 9    - Didsbury at Didsbury
"    " 20  - Cheshire County at Chelford
"    " 23  - Clifford at Old Trafford
June 6    - Ashton at Stockport
"    " 13  - Rusholme at Rusholme
"    " 20  - Longsight at Stockport
"    " 27  - Werneth at Werneth
July 4    - Clifford at Stockport
"    " 11  - Sale at Sale
"    " 25  - Ashton at Ashton
Aug 1    - Rusholme at Stockport
"    " 15  - Werneth at Stockport
"    " 22  - Didsbury at Stockport
"    " 29  - Levenshulme at Levenshulme
Sept 5   - Sale at Stockport
"    " 12  - Longsight at Longsight
*N.B. - All Club and Ground except Sale.*

### BOWLING MATCHES

June 20  - Longsight at Stockport
July 4   - Reddish at Reddish
This Card does not admit to the Athletic Sports

The Second X1 fixtures were a reversal of the First Team on the same day.

No doubt, many cricket lovers have heard the famous story of W.G. Grace: The young fast bowler raced in and bowled the doctor early in the match, but the umpire immediately declared 'not out'. When the bowler complained to the umpire he said: 'See here young feller th' crowds come to see Dr. Grace's batting not thy bowling'! Dr. Grace was bowled by McIntyre in the first over, but was allowed to continue to the great delight of the vast number of spectators! The doctor stayed at the nearby 'Blossoms Hotel', where a plaque recorded the event.

On August 31st, 1st & 2nd September, 1876 - the first match v the United South of England X1, including W.G. Grace, then at the height of his fame, was played upon the ground at Higher Hillgate. This game excited great interest in the town and neighbourhood and raised £62 16s. to the funds of the club. The 22 players who represented Stockport, scored 224 in the first innings - the scores of the Southern X1 were 55 and 238 (W.G. Grace 133).

**The famous match when the W.G. Grace incident took place was on June 14th, 15th & 16th 1877,** when the United South X1 again visited Stockport - this time, victory for the Southerners: Stockport's 22 players scored 91and 267, South X1 255 (W.G. Grace 124) and 104, for the loss of 6 wickets. A crowd of nearly 2,000 witnessed the game - Mr. D. Fletcher of the 'Blossoms Hotel' looked after the catering, placing 2 canvas tents in different parts of the ground. The financial result of this match was a profit of £30 6s. 4d.

In both 1878 and 1880, Stockport were given the honour of hosting the touring Australian Test side as part of their UK visit. On the first tour, the Australians won the match - played on July 4th, 5th & 6th, 1878, 16 of Stockport plus professionals W.R. Gilbert and McIntyre scored 105 & 184, Australian X1 163 & 225. To accommodate the large crowd, seats were placed all round the ground. Two large refreshment tents were included - one looked after by Mr. Fletcher of the 'Blossoms' and the other by Mr. Worthington of the 'Red Bull'. Due to the importance of the game, it was given 2 full columns of match reports!

 The Australian's also defeated England in the only Test Match at Lords - the MCC scored 33 and 19 all out, the Australians 41 all out and 12 for 1 - must be the lowest scoring Test on record!

The second tour in 1880 saw England win the only Test at the Oval, and in the game on the 26th, 27th and 28th August at Charles Street, the 18 of Stockport and District beat the Australian X1. Apart from the advantage of fielding an extra 7 players, the Stockport side also included the services of 3 Yorkshire players: Tom Emmett, a current Test player at the time, Billy

W.G. Grace played twice v Stockport CC in the 1870s

Bates, who took England's first Test hat-trick and Allen Hill, who both played and umpired Test cricket - all 3 made some good scores and bowled out the Australians between them in the 2nd innings.. The match ball from this historic match is displayed along with the scorecard in the club pavilion. The Scorecard is copied below:

One of the great local names with Stockport Cricket Club, was James Horner, a JP, who played against the Australians and was not out on 4 occasions! He was

## GRAND CRICKET MATCH

## AUSTRALIAN ELEVEN v. 18 OF STOCKPORT AND DISTRICT

| STOCKPORT | 1st Innings | 2nd Innings |
|---|---|---|
| 11 Mr. A. McLachlin | c. Alexander, b. Boyle ............................0 | c. Moule, b. Boyle ............................29 |
| 1 Mr. G.Pearson | c. Moule, b. Boyle ...........................30 | c and b Palmer.................................0 |
| 4 T Emmett | c. Jarvis, b. Boyle ............................22 | c. Bonner, b. Palmer ........................0 |
| 5 W Bates | b. Alexander ........................................0 | c. Groube, b. Boyle .........................23 |
| 12 A Hill | c. Moule, b. Boyle ..............................1 | b. Palmer ..........................................14 |
| 6 T Brown | c. Palmer, b. Alexander ........................0 | c. McDonnell, b Alexander .............8 |
| 7 T Whatmough | c. Torkington, b. Alexander ..............21 | c. Slight, b. Boyle ............................22 |
| 8 Mr. JF Cryer | b. Alexander ........................................0 | c. Slight, b. Boyle .............................5 |
| 10 Mr. S Hollins | c. sub. B. Alexander ............................3 | st. Jarvis, b. Boyle ............................0 |
| 9 Mr. RG Challinor | st. Jarvis, b Boyle ............................20 | c. Alexander, b. Boyle ......................2 |
| 3 Mr. WS Mills | c. McDonnell, b. Alexander ...............0 | c. McDonnell, b. Boyle ....................9 |
| 16 Mr. HP Boulton | b. Alexander ........................................0 | c. McDonnell, b. Boyle ....................8 |
| 2 Mr. GL Vaughan | b. Boyle ...............................................6 | b. Boyle ............................................15 |
| 13 Mr. FM Jackson | c. Boyle, b. Alexander .........................6 | c. Bannerman, b. Boyle ...................1 |
| 14 Mr. W Emery | c. Palmer, b. Boyle ...........................10 | c. Alexander, b. Boyle ......................0 |
| 15 Mr. T Marsland | c. Groube, b. Boyle .............................3 | c. McDonnell, b. Boyle ....................4 |
| 17 Mr. H Torkington | c. Alexander, b. Boyle .........................0 | c. Moule, b. Boyle ............................0 |
| 18 Mr. J Horner | not out ................................................0 | not out ...............................................2 |
| | 9 byes, 1lb ........................................10 | 10 byes, 4 lb .....................................14 |
| | **132** | **156** |

| AUSTRALIANS | 1st Innings | | 2nd Innings | |
|---|---|---|---|---|
| 5 WL Murdoch | c. Hill, b. Bates | 29 | c. Brown, b. Emmett | 12 |
| 2 AC Bannerman | c and b Hill | 8 | Hurt | 6 |
| 3 TU Groube | Hit wicket, b Brown | 15 | b. Emmett | 10 |
| 4 PS McDonnell | c. Whatmough, b Brown | 4 | b. Emmett | 5 |
| 9 GE Palmer | c. McLachlan, b. Brown | 1 | b. Bates | 0 |
| 8 GJ Bonner | b. Hill | 0 | b. Emmett | 1 |
| 10 HF Boyle | c. Cryer, b. Bates | 2 | Not Out | 17 |
| 1 G Alexander | c. Whatmough, b. Bates | 0 | c. Jackson, b. Emmett | 21 |
| 11 WH Moule | b. Hill | 3 | b. Hill | 3 |
| 7 J Slight | Run out | 0 | b. Hill | 29 |
| 6 AH Jarvis | Not out | 0 | b. Bates | 1 |
| | 1 wd, 3 byes, 4lb | 8 | 1 wd, 12 byes | 13 |
| | | **70** | | **118** |

**Umpires** - Messrs Howarth and Greenwood

**Note**: Only 'gentlemen' players had 'Mr.' before their name!

connected with the club since 1872, and Honorary Secretary for 52 years, being also an Honorary Treasurer for Lancashire for 10 years.

Another personality of the early history was Sam Brown, formerly of Nottinghamshire, who was professional for the club. Local tradition holds that he once drove a ball through the pavilion clock and his best innings was his 101 not out v Winnington Park at the ripe old age of 57!

There was a further International match in 1880 with a team of Canadians, who, as the result proved, had been ill-advised in coming to England to play cricket - their performances were by no means equal to what had been expected from them. The game was played 12 aside, the result being: Stockport, first innings 196; Canadians, first innings, 90; second innings, 101 -

also a financial failure!

At the end of June in 1883, Stockport Cricket Club opened their new ground at Cale Green with a match v Sale. A section of the report of the proceedings:

*CRICKET*
*OPENING OF THE NEW GROUND AT*
*STOCKPORT*

*'The new ground of Stockport Cricket Club was opened on Saturday. As stated in previous issues of this journal, the new ground forms a part of the Cale Green Estate, and consists of about seven acres of land purchased from Mr. S.R. Carrington, J.P., for a little more than £2300. The principal approaches are from Adswood-lane and Cale Green, and we understand that the London and North-Western Railway Company, whose line to Buxton runs along*

W.G. Grace (third left) with the England Cricket team

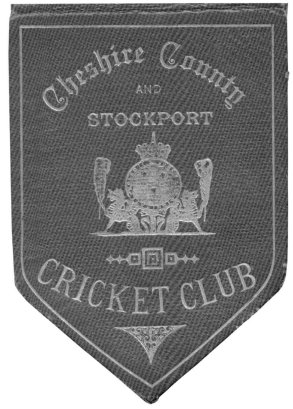

the westerly side, have consented to a path being made from Garner's-lane, which will give ready access to the ground to persons arriving at Davenport Station and to the inhabitants of the rapidly-increasing neighbourhood of Bramhall-lane.

The expenses of levelling and preparing the land, constructing a bowling green, and providing the necessary erections, have made the total cost into something over £4000. The promoters of the undertaking have confidence that the public will attend the new ground in sufficient numbers to enable them gradually to liquidate the liabilities they have incurred, especially as the new ground is to be placed on such a basis as shall secure its permanent use for the purpose to which it has now been devoted.

We are pleased to say that the large attendances on the opening day afforded gentlemen who had been foremost in the undertaking the greatest encouragement. The presence of so many ladies also was a very gratifying feature, and, we hope, may be taken as an augury of success. The Mayor (Mr James Leigh, J.P.) president of the club, was there, and the Mayoress, also Lieut. - col. Mc.Clure, J.P., Major Howard, J.P., Mr Henry Bell, J.P., Mr. Joseph Leigh, J.P., and all the habitués of the old ground; whilst amongst the visitors from a distance may be mentioned Major Dixon of Chelford, treasurer and joint hon. secretary with Mr James Horner of the Cheshire County Club.

Of the general public there was a splendid muster, and on all hands might be heard expressions which clearly indicated thorough appreciation of the new ground and its surroundings. The feeling of admiration will be heightened when the new pavilion is completed, and when terraces have been formed in front of the handsome structure, as from this point there is obtained an extensive view of the vale of

Cheshire, and of the high land in the neighbourhood of Alderley, Lyme, Bollington, Marple, and Werneth'.

For the record, the match was a draw - Stockport 138, Sale 62 for 7 at close of play.

The amount paid for the land was £2,382, and the cost of making, levelling, fencing, and other charges was £895. Towards this amount, through the generosity of the members and other friends, by the proceeds of Trotting (horses) Races, and a Calico Ball (a ball at which ladies wear cotton dresses), enabled the handsome sum of £1,486 to be collected - a further sum of £1,500 was obtained by mortgage, and the balance of £291 was secured by an overdraft at the bank.

Having acquired and laid out the ground, steps were next taken to erect a Pavilion, and as a result of a competition, the designs of Messrs Preston & Vaughan were accepted. The contractor, Edward Barlow completed the work, slightly under £1,000. To raise the funds, a Grand Bazaar was held at the Armoury, Greek Street, on May 3rd, 4th, and 5th, 1883 - it was enthusiastically supported by the whole town, and the result, a net profit of £1,012 6s.

At the AGM, in November 1883, a resolution was passed that the club should amalgamate with the Cheshire County Cricket Club - in order to promote County Cricket. The club was now called the Cheshire County & Stockport Cricket Club. Previously, there had been a Cheshire County Club so called, whose headquarters were at Chelford - although a small village, it had a big cricket pitch!

This was not, in any way a representative County Team, but rather a Cheshire County Gentlemen's Club - however in 1883, Cheshire were, for example, entertaining Warwickshire. It was with full consent of the Chelford Club, as also of other clubs in the County. This agreement stayed in place up to the end of 1891, when, owing to the excessive annual loss incurred chiefly through not receiving the full support of the clubs at the West end of the County, it was decided to drop County Cricket as part of the Stockport Club. County Cricket was to continue on a

separate basis, detached from any particular club and was better supported by the County.

Owing to its establishment in new quarters, and giving greater convenience to members, and also the prestige caused by being amalgamated with the County Club, the membership increased during 1883-84 from about 300 to over 500. In spite of this, so heavy were the expenses of a new ground, and the loss incurred by pursing County Cricket, that in 1886 there was in addition to the mortgage of £1,500, an overdraft at the bank of £460. Owing, however, to special efforts on behalf of the County and reducing the number of County matches played, this adverse balance was very considerably reduced.

The Stockport Club had every reason to remember with gratitude, the support it received during its management of County Cricket from H. Thornber, Esq., as representing the Sale Club, and from Colonel Dixon.

In October 1884, the whole of the property was conveyed to a number of Trustees. The Trust Deed provided that when the Trustees are reduced to 12, 16 additional Trustees must be appointed, half by the existing Trustees, and the other half by the members of the club. It also provides that if at any time the Cricket Club shall be unable or unwilling to maintain the ground and Club premises for playing cricket, the Trustees may maintain same and allow them to be used for some other outdoor game or for amateur athletics, subject to proper rules!

Members Card 1894 front, back & inside

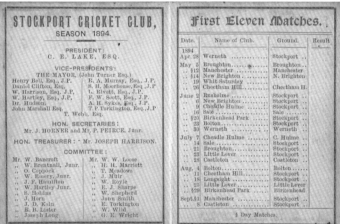

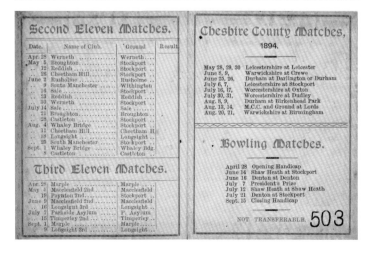

In June, 1885, Lancashire sent a team to play Cheshire at Cale Green. Lancashire bowler, Johnny Crossland had in one season claimed 97 wickets at only 10 runs each, but many counties complained about his bowling action - Lord Harris of Kent refused to have Crossland in his England team! This game at Stockport was his last, before enforced retirement from first-class cricket.

At the Annual Dinner in December, 1886, the opportunity was taken up to present to the then Councillor T.P. Torkington, a portrait of himself, painted by A.H. Fox. For 13 years, Mr. Torkington was Treasurer to the Cricket Club - during this period the club had to establish itself on its new ground, with all the financial implications involved.

In the spring of 1888, the land on the West side of the Cricket Ground was purchased along with other land, by Mr. Henry Wild with the object of building cottages there. With a view to preventing this, and also with a view for future extension of the ground, the club approached Mr. Wild and bought from him with favourable terms, an extra 2 and a half acres of land. The total cost of this ground, and levelling and fencing it in, was £1,317 - of this sum £800 was obtained on mortgage, and the balance of £517 was raised by donations from members and friends.

The AGM held in the pavilion in November 1888 had an extra important subject on the agenda, Rugby Football! It was agreed this new land would be used for the next 3 winter months. New Rule 21: There shall be a Football Club, to which the following rules shall apply:-

(a) *The club shall be called 'The Stockport Football Club'.*

(b) *'The subscription for the season shall be not less than 3s (15p) for each member - Life Members and Annual Subscribers of not less that £1 1s. to the Cricket Club shall, without any additional subscription, be members of the Football Club'.*

(c) *'The Game shall be played according to the Rules of the 'Rugby Union'.'*

(d) *'The General Committee of the Cricket Club shall have absolute control over all financial matters; and the Honorary Treasurer of the Cricket Club for the time being shall be the Honorary Treasurer of the Football Club.*

(e) *'The Committee of the Football Club shall consist of the ex-officio members and four members selected by the General Committee of the Cricket Club, together with twelve other members to be elected annually by the Football Club, of whom not less than two-thirds shall be football players; and such Committee shall have power to arrange all Football Matches, select teams, and appoint the Captains of the same, but in all other respects shall be a Sub-Committee of the General Committee of the Cricket Club'.*

In 1890, the frequent overcrowding of the Bowling Green led to a proposal by bowling members for an additional Green - the club acquired sufficient land on lease from Messrs. Carrington and created a new Green of larger dimensions. The total cost of this, in addition to the annual ground rent of £11, was £130. 'The desirability of having Bowling Greens in connection with Cricket Clubs is shown by the fact that a great number of our present trundlers are those who formerly played cricket, but having become too old or too stiff for that game, have retained their membership and connection with the club by the Bowling Green'.

To give you some idea of the strength of Stockport C.C., in Season 1891 and 1892, the Second X1 completed all their matches undefeated!

There was a 'novel' cricket match staged at Cale Green in the summer of 1892, **LADIES v GENTLEMEN**. It was certainly very early days for ladies cricket - the handicap for the men: bat with a broomstick and bowl and catch with their left hand! The scores were: Ladies 59, Gentlemen 43.

The Stockport Bowling Club at Cale Green by 1900, had built up a very large membership. The Presidents' Prize attracted sufficient competitors for 51 matches in the first round. The final was between W. Brewster (11) v T. Chorlton (10).

Stockport CC had 3 professionals in their ranks for the summer of 1900 - Brown, Disney and Cooper. There was a benefit match for them, held in August: Stockport 126, Manchester 45 for 5 at stumps.

The village of Davenport developed when the railway station was built, and between 1880 - 1914 there was a building boom in this area. The region known as Cale Green, was originally the Cale Green Estate, a country estate owned by the aristocratic Davenport family. The estate was sold off in the late 1890s, and most of the land was built upon.

Mr. Henry Bell, who owned Bell's Brewery on Hempshaw Lane, was a magistrate and Alderman of Stockport and in 1907, the Mayor, as well as President of the Cricket Club. When the piece of land adjoining the cricket club was under threat for building, the members of the club sought to save it and approached Henry Bell to see if he could buy the land and lease it to the cricket club - to keep it as an open space, near to where he had his own fine house. Bell purchased the land for £3,500 and offered it to the public as a free gift - on the provision that it should be laid out as a public recreation ground, named Cale Green Park and opened in 1902.

Stockport Cricket Club collected £500 from local residents to pay for the fencing of the park, and raised £600 from its own members to pay for the purchase of 2 further parts of land, now within its own site and used for bowling and lacrosse.

The A.G.M. of 1907 was held in the Pavilion at Cale Green. Mr. F.S. Tyler (hon. Secretary) read the annual report. The first X1 played 20 matches during the season, 12 were won, 5 drawn and 3 lost. The second X1 played 16, won 11, 3 drawn and 2 lost. Dr. Bailey won the gold medal with batting average of 21.58, the highest average for the previous year was 38.25. Dr. Bailey also won the bowling prize for the fourth time in succession, with an average of 16.14.

Bowling matches were played with the Shaw Heath, Severnside (Shrewsbury), and Victoria clubs. Two were won and one drawn.

The balance sheet was submitted for the past year. The revenue showed that the wages, travelling expenses, umpires, scorers and police service had cost £379 10s 4d; rates, taxes, gas, water, insurance and telephone rent £116 1s 11d; repairs, painting, whitewashing, plumbing etc. £193 9s 3d; cricket material etc. £27 11s 9d; printing, stationery, stamps etc. £28 13s 4d; batting and bowling prizes £11 7s 8d; total expenditure including smaller items £808 7s 8d.

The receipts including subscriptions £493 18s 6d; gate money (cricket & lacrosse) £41 0s 7d; Stockport Lacrosse Club £20; bar £159 1s 4d; the balance to profit and loss account being £94 7s 3d. The

Stockport Cricket Club. 1st Eleven. 1904.

membership of the club was not as big as it used to be, so the membership fee of 10s 6d was removed.

**Cheadle Hulme School**'s origins go back to **1855 -** initially formed as The Manchester Warehousemen and Clerks' Orphan Schools, with just 6 pupils. In the 1850's, life expectancy for those working in the inner-cities was very poor, and many were worried what would happen to their children should their father die. Pupils were first sent to a school in Shaw Hall, Flixton - 6 years later moving to its own rented premises at Park Place, Ardwick. Paying day pupils were accepted during the school's time at Ardwick.

The Mayor of Manchester granted the children the use of a field, at the back of the Polygon, in which to play. It resulted with the boys having their own cricket club - the Committee challenged the boys to a match, but the older men had an 'easy victory'.

It was decided that a new school should be built and the foundation stone at its present site in Cheadle Hulme was laid in 1867, moving 2 years later. Since the beginning, it was a boarding school for the orphans, linked to fathers who worked in Manchester's warehouses.

'Tennis Lawn' at Cheadle Hulme School in 1916

A Gymnasium was one of the first sporting facilities to be built at Cheadle Hulme in 1871. The boys' and girls' play was segregated. They had separate playrooms inside the school, in the school yard and, separate fields outside to play on. There must have been very few schools that had their own swimming baths, but this major development was completed in 1876. A 'dressing room' was added in 1887, but heating of the baths was not considered until 1905 - the water must have been 'freezing' for the pupils! The baths were enlarged in 1898 but not used by the girls until 1900 - it had been considered unladylike! By 1903, 80% of the 157 boys and 70% of the 79 girls could swim. Maintaining the bath was a constant problem, largely due to the difficulties of obtaining clean water from Stockport Corporation.

The Boys' playing field was located away from the school grounds, which were still very small, despite attempts by the Committee to buy more land. The field was rented from the Countess of Dundonald and was reached by going under the railway bridge and turning left behind Heathbank Road.

A James Buckley remembered getting into trouble on his first day for playing cricket in the playground: 'We had not been playing more than a few minutes when Goodier, with a high drive to the off, knocked the ball out of the playground, and through the first window of the first floor room of the main building'. James recalled his Saturday cricket fondly, played on the field behind Heathbank Road.

**'There were three grounds, first, second and third, and I naturally belonged to the third for the same reason that made the bishop travel third class on the railway - because there was no fourth. Arthur Williams, who eventually became the shining light of the first eleven, was at that time on the third ground, and took most of our wickets with what appeared to us to be very fast underhands. Overarm bowling had only recently been permitted by the M.C.C., and at school we were still living under the rule which did not permit the hand higher than the shoulder when the ball was delivered.'**

The first reported cricket match for the school was in 1872 v Longsight Juniors, played and won at Cheadle Hulme by Warehousemen & Clerks'. Soon after followed a game v Heaton Chapel Juniors, scores: Cheadle Hulme 93, Heaton Chapel 79.

A news item in August 1875, included the first reference of an Old Boys cricket match - Warehousemen & Clerks' 85 runs, Old Boys 70.

Football was introduced to the school, many years before Rugby appeared. Norman Hayward recalled his playtime fondly:

**'My mind reverts back to multitudes of happy incidents and customs, games of football after tea and before 'prep' about 50 a-side, a rough and tumble affair where one side elected to be Oxford University and the other Cambridge. I generally favoured the light blues, but when we came to wash for 'prep' we were all blacks, or black and blue!'**

Girls Hockey Team at Cheadle Hulme School c1910

Lacrosse had started in Stockport in the 1870s and was being added to the sports at many schools in North East Cheshire, Warehouseman and Clerks was one of them. The lacrosse team had a treat in 1902 of watching the Toronto touring team v Cheshire at Cale Green.

Girls also played sport i.e. Tennis, Croquet was available in the 1880s. In 1900, when Woods Field was rented, they also learnt to play Hockey. Mr. Board (headmaster) went to town himself to buy 36 hockey sticks, and then 3 years later, the Old Girls Association donated a further 6 hockey sticks and a ball. The 1905 Annual Report also declared that the girls played Cricket as well, again the Old Girls donated the necessary equipment. Netball was another sport introduced for the young ladies of the school.

The 1905 Sports Day, was given great prominence by the *Stockport Advertiser*, including a drawing of the original school buildings. The children's events included flat races for boys and girls, as well as a Jockey race for the boys, an egg and spoon race for the girls, a sack race and 3 legged race. A cricket match was staged, Past v Present. After the cricket and sports were over, there was tea and then speeches by the Committee and the Old Scholars' Associations, followed by a prize giving.

In 1911, a new swimming pool was planned and 2 foundation stones laid. The new pool was to be 75 feet long by 25 feet wide with a capacity of 60,000 gallons of water. To help supply the water, an artesian well was sunk to a depth of 365 feet. - producing 3,000 gallons of water per hour. The pump room was in a building next to the current tennis courts. The old bath was converted to a new gymnasium.

Throughout this period there was tremendous emphasis placed on the all round well being of the children. The Annual Report of 1910 stressed that, '....the combination of the mental and the physical is carefully balanced.' The shorter school hours were to allow for more sports and other non-academic pursuits. Daily Swedish Drill was introduced for the girls. The new swimming bath and gymnasium were extensively used. There were great sporting successes, particularly in lacrosse.

The first issue of a school magazine was printed in 1914 and the sporting life of the school was recorded in it. It reported:

'It is gratifying to note with what keenness Cricket is now being played on the special pitches for each of the six houses and practically all the boys may be seen playing on the field at one time'.

The Houses were named after important benefactors; Rylands, Matheson, Holden, Broome, Milner and Gledhill.

Football had always been played for fun in the school but now introduced as an 'official' sport, to separate the boys' and girls' fields. The magazine quoted;

'The time honoured contest between Oxford and Cambridge proceeded vigorously from the beginning of term. As usual the daily football matches in the yard created universal enthusiasm and the party feeling often ran high'.

**Didsbury Cricket Club** is one of the oldest in the area, dating back to its foundation in **1858**. The club originally played on a leased ground now partly covered by Beaver Road School. This land was sold for housing development at the end of the 19th century, forcing a move to the present site at East Didsbury.

One of the pavilions that was built, a wooden one, opened in 1900, and lasted until it was destroyed in an arson attack in 1981 - sadly a lot of the club's history went in the fire.

One of the most important officials of the Didsbury Club in the first half of the 20th Century, was George Harold White. He was Treasurer from 1902-4, Secretary 1905-35 and Captain of the 1st Team from 1911-27. From 1900 onwards, Mr. White was to be a member of the club for 50 years!

The new ground was also on lease and the owners later decided to sell it, again for housing. Having nowhere else to go, the club developed a plan to buy the land by forming the Didsbury Cricket Club Ground Company Ltd - mainly members bought shares.. The required sum of £1,700 was raised to make the purchase and the ground company still exists today.

In the late 1850s, there were several new cricket clubs starting up in the Stockport area. One of which was the Alma Club, which played at Green Lane, Heaton Norris - their team was strong enough to play Stockport's 2nd X1. Other early clubs on the scene were: Royal George (Stockport), Portwood Trades, Wellington Club (Hazel Grove), Davenport, India Mill, Brinnington, Cheadle Village, Bow Garretts Perserverance, Edgeley Royal Albert (played on a field adjoining Edgeley House, lent by Richard Sykes Esq.), Lancashire Hill, Brunswick & Wellington, Heaton Mersey Grundy Hill and Heaton Mersey Trades.

Matches between these teams could be either one or two innings length, and if there was insufficient time to finish a 2 innings encounter, the best 1st innings score would establish the winner!

By 1860, there were no longer any reports of Horse Racing meetings in the press, so we can only assume that the local courses now ceased to exist. In the winter months, there was no sport reported - Football or Rugby not yet featured!

Stockport's first ever Bowling Green opened in **Vernon Park** in **1860** and Victoria Bowling Club having an oval green on the Woodbank side of the Museum.

In 1861, the Charlestown Club opened up their cricket season on April 2nd with a game between their two elevens - Mr. R. Pidgeon's side scored 53 and Mr. J. Marsden 52. Life in this Victorian period was very comfortable for members of the 'gentleman's' clubs, an abstract from the match report:

**'After stumps were drawn the combatants adjourned to the house of Mr. Mark Minshull, when a good substantial dinner was served up to which the fatigues of the day, all parties did ample justice. After the cloth was drawn a variety of toasts, recitations songs, & c. were given, and then dancing commenced and was kept up with the spirit till late hour, when the company separated, each person highly gratified with the days proceedings'.**

**Heaton Norris Cricket Club** dates back to c. **1860**, their first match traced was in 1862 v Charlestown. The club played for many years at the 'Ash Inn' ground on Manchester Road, Heaton Chapel - A Tithe map from 1848 shows a Bowling Green and Gardens plus a field owned by a William Higginbotham, where cricket and football were to be played in the future, next to the Inn. By 1875, the club was considered important enough to have their seasons fixtures published:

Heaton Norris CC played Stockport for several summers and the latter usually got the better of them. However, in 1875, the scores read: Heaton Norris 79 runs, Stockport 22 and 22 for 5 - the former winning on 1st innings. A usual inclusion at a cricket match in this period was a brass band, this game was no exception - Heaton Mersey Brass Band provided an 'excellent selection of music' before a 'large collection of ladies and gentlemen of the district'. 'After the game a handsome collection was made for the Heaton Norris professional* for his excellent bowling, which he duly acknowledged'. * F. Watson.

| | | |
|---|---|---|
| May | 1 | Cheetham (home) |
| " " | 8 | Manchester Clifford (Old Trafford) |
| " " | 15 | Gorton (home) |
| " " | 22 | Whit Saturday |
| June | 5 | Beswick (away) |
| " " | 12 | Sandbach (away) (Day Match) |
| " " | 19 | Birch (away) |
| " " | 26 | Manchester Clifford (home) |
| July | 3 | Crewe (home) |
| " " | 10 | Stockport (home) |
| " " | 17 | Fallow field (away) |
| " " | 24 | Bradford & Clayton (Clayton) |
| " " | 31 | — |
| Aug | 7 | Sandbach (home) (Day Match) |
| " " | 14 | Birch (away) |
| " " | 21 | Gorton (away) |
| " " | 28 | Beswick (away) |
| Sep | 4 | Cheetham (away) |
| " " | 11 | Stockport (away) |
| " " | 18 | Crewe (away) |

To prove this match was no fluke, the following season, Heaton Norris (87 runs) defeated one of the premier clubs in Cheshire, Macclesfield (52), to show they were one of the best teams in town!

By the mid 1890s, Heaton Norris Cricket Club had folded - probably due to dwindling membership, as there were now numerous other teams playing in the area. The ground was still used for some football matches i.e. Stockport & District Cup semi-final in 1896-97.

In the summer of 1904, there was a reformed Heaton Norris CC playing at Stockport County's old ground, Green Lane and were still there at the outbreak of World War 1.

**Marple Cricket Club** came into existence at least as long ago as **1864**, when the first reported match was v the 14 players of Marple Academy. The latter's team consisted of 2 masters, 3 old pupils and 9 present students. The game was played on the Marple CC ground, which was sited below the 'Railway Hotel', Stockport Road, now occupied by Oak Drive, Kays Wood Road, Beech Avenue and Hawthorn Avenue.

In 1874, Marple (80 runs) staged a local match on Bank holiday Monday v Brabins Hall (49) before a large crowd. Shortly before this game Brabins scored 68 v Godley United (34), T. Thorniley scored 43 of the runs, with extras 9, next highest score! Another game this season was: Marple 63 runs v Copley Hall 67. An early example of a scorecard being published in the 'Stockport Advertiser' in May 1879, reflects their match away to Poynton, who scored 108 to Marple's 57. In 1882 the club appears to be referred to as Rose Hill (Marple), in another game away to Poynton Vernon.

In 1898, Marple played one of their first matches v Compstall - not surprisingly, Marple (90) were far too strong for Compstall (37).

The club folded during World War 1, and their pavilion was sold to Hazel Grove CC. Marple Cricket Club didn't reform until as late as 1950, with a new home off Bowden Lane.

By the mid 1860's, there was a further 'wave' of cricket clubs appearing on the scene: Disley, Edgeley Victoria, Mount Tabor (Adswood), Hawk Green, Hollins Mill, Egerton Club, St. Mary's & St. Thomas's, Stockport Moor, Waterside Victoria (Disley), Stockport Sunday School Improvement,* Heaton Norris Egerton, Heaviley, Christ Church, Stockport West End and High Lane. Many of these team were no doubt short lived or only played a hand full of matches in a season. **\*There were several teams with the word 'Improvement' in their title - 'A worker who accepts low wages in order to learn a trade, especially in millinery'.**

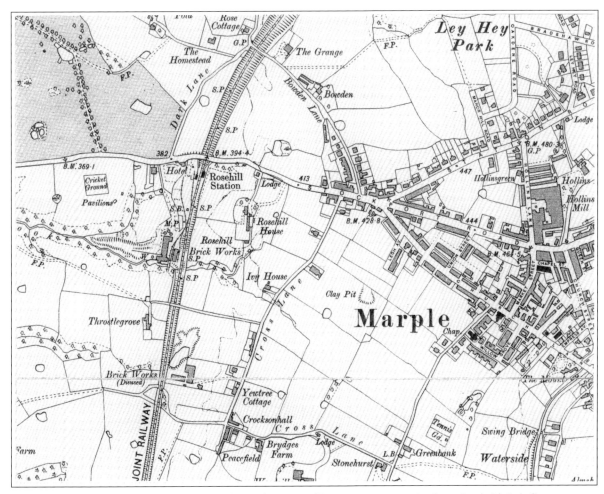

The site of the original Marple Cricket Club can be seen on this 1890s map, next to Stockport Road with 2 pavilions

At Cheadle, in February 1870, we have the first reference to ice skating. Mrs. Milnes' large pond at Belmont was open to everyone. Many people took advantage of the offer: 'Evening fires and torches brought light along the pond - it is pleasing to see that all passed without accident'.

In nearby Gatley, the same year, another pastime was Sparrow Shooting. The prize being a Copper Kettle provided by Mr. Moult, the proprietor of the 'Prince of Wales'. The entrance fee was 2/- (10p) - the winner being the person who killed and gathered the largest number of sparrows within the boundary out of six. Nine competitors took part, 2 men killed 4 each, but the winner was a Mr. Lane, killing 5 birds!

Pigeon shooting was also taking place in Gatley in a field adjoining the 'Horse and Farrier'. The fee to enter was £2 and Mr. Mills won the competition, having 'brought six to ground'.

At Marple there was a Bowling Match taking place on the bowling green behind the 'Jolly Sailor'. First prize was a copper tea kettle, given by the landlady Mrs. Shirley to the winner, Mr. F. Tetlow.

Cricket clubs included in the local press for the first time in 1870 were: Heaton Chapel, Hempshaw Lane, Royal Portwood, New Mills, Daw Bank, Norbury,

Stockport Original, Shaw Heath United, Cheadle Heath, Mellor and Bredbury

Stockport Anglers Preservation Society in 1872, staged their first fishing excursion at High Lane canal. The contest was for a fishing rod valued at 10s 6d, second prize was 5s - the latter subscribed by those competing. Few fish were caught, and those that were, on the small side! Mr. Harrison, a manufacturer, was declared the winner - the next contest was to be on the Reddish canal.

The bowling section of Stockport CC had a match v Reddish at the 'Houldsworth Arms Hotel', Reddish. **Doubles: Stockport 67, Reddish 70 - Singles: Stockport 95, Reddish 126 - Reddish won by 34.**

Bowling had now become very popular in the Stockport area, Heaton Chapel were playing Levenshulme at the 'Chapel House' with 16 on each team. **Doubles: Heaton Chapel 60, Levenshlume 44 - Singles: Heaton Chapel 122, Levenshulme 84 - Chapel won by 54.** A report of the game:

**'Members of both clubs and visitors partook of a first class Te La Fourchette in the large room of the Chapel House, furnished by Mr. Charles Crush the worthy proprietor. The repost consisted of poultry and fish in season and was most elaborately served.**

Many songs were given, toasts proposed and responded to. For the convenience of the Levenshulme gentlemen special conveyances were retained'

The 'Windsor Castle' green at Edgeley were hosting a tournament, 1st prize was a handsome pair of bowls made in Manchester plus 3 money prizes - 32 bowlers took part, spread over 2 days.

**Alderley Edge Cricket Club** was founded in **1872.** The club very quickly created interest in the village, and by 1874 had attracted 160 members - the ground was described as 'one of the most beautifully situated grounds in the Kingdom'! The first match traced in the press appeared in July 1872 - a very brief report stating that Alderley scored 75 to Ashton's 136.

A Bowling Green was laid at a cost of £90 within 2 years. In order to improve the bowling facilities, a concert was held at Chorley Church - many artistes agreed to appear, in what was a very successful evening. The start of the 1874 season, saw a match between the 'Bachelors' (96 runs) v Benedicts (newly married men) (70). Alderley were well beaten, when they played against Ashbourne, scoring 20 and 32 to Ashbourne's 96. The following day, victory: Alderley Edge 121, Sale 53.

In 1875, Alderley played what would be the first of many matches against Bowden, scores: Alderley 65 runs, Bowden 77.

In July 1912, the annual Alderley Edge Lawn Tennis Tournament was held - consisting of mixed doubles, ladies' doubles, ladies' singles, men's doubles and men's singles. Mrs. S.A. Bennett presented the prizes.

Although the F.A. had been formed back in 1863, sets of rules in place and the game becoming popular, there was still no mention of Association Football in the local press. By now, in some towns, Old Boys from Universities or Public Schools had returned home to form clubs and play the game experienced during their education.

**The first time Rugby was reported, was in November 1872.** There was a match at Didsbury, Free Wanderers v Levenshulme. The same day, Alderley were playing the Northenden Road Club - an easy victory for the former. As in the early days of cricket, the number of players in a side was not set in stone. Levenshulme's next game v Clarendon featured 20 players per team. In 1863, there had been a basic split between Association Football and Rugby but there were still different interpretations of the rules!

When Levenshulme were up against St. Michael's at Moss Side, the teams fielded 17 players. Judging by the report of the match, we find Rugby with an element of football - St. Michael's won by 3 rouges and 1 try to Levenshulme's 3 rouges.

The 'Rouge' was adopted by the scholars at Eton, a method of forcing a goal by having an area 4 yards on either side of the goal marked with flags. Players were awarded a point for touching the ball down within or kicking it through these spaces. In the association game, a goal outweighs any number of rouges, if the goals scored was equal, the match was decided by this method. Although it was never accepted by the F.A., it was used for many years in one of the most important early development areas for football - the Sheffield Association.

The home team could sometimes decide the exact rules to adopt - when Levenshulme played Altrincham, they stated that no 'hacking' (kicking a player's shins) was allowed. Until half-time, Levenshulme could only muster 9 men!

**West Heaton Bowling Club** was founded on 11th July **1873**, becoming one of the oldest in the Stockport area. The founders obtained a lease of the present grounds for 21 years. The first President was W. Romaine Callender Esq. M.P., a well known citizen of Manchester and a local resident.

On the 24th July 1873, a bowling green and croquet lawn were opened. As early as 1875, a bowling tournament was held in which 13 members played - 6 years later a Bowling Captain was appointed.

The new game of tennis soon created interest, and a 'tennis lawn' was in place by 1880, adjoining the bowling green at a cost of £15 - one of the first tennis clubs in Stockport. In May 1881, those participating were urged to provide themselves with tennis shoes when the new 'lawn tennis ground' was opened. The following year, saw a 'cinder rink' (hard court) laid near the entrance in Princes Road. By 1882, 'croquet has been little practised this year' - due to the demand for tennis, the area was converted for lawn tennis.

A Pavilion was erected in 1888 at a cost of £80, which helped create a very active social side. The club was honoured in 1902 and 1903, when 3 members were included in the Manchester & District team. Followed in 1904, by Percy Brownsword and Cluny Millar winning the Lancashire County Doubles Championship.

At the end of the century, the lease expired and was renewed yearly. More accommodation followed in 1905, costing £160 and some years later, the land was purchased for £450 and £5 shares in the Limited Company were issued to members.

A remarkable pair of bowls with expensive silver mounts, far larger than modern crown green bowls, were discovered in the 1980s in an attic in Oundle near Peterborough and eventually returned to the West Heaton club. The bowls had been won by a Mr. A. Adam back in 1886 and passed down to his grand-daughter - the bowls are still used on the official opening day each spring!

Until now, any rugby reports were 'tucked away' on the district news pages but in February, 1874, Football actually had its own heading! The matches all appear to be rugby: Wellington 1st 15 with 2 goals, 2 touchdowns, 3 rouges, defeated Burnage 1 goal, 1 try. Stockport Crusaders, 1 try, 1 touchdown, 2 rouges v Bowdon College F.C., 1 goal, 1 try, 2 touchdowns, 3 rouges.

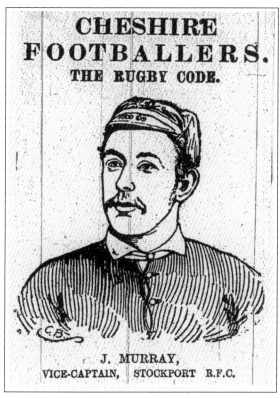

CHESHIRE
FOOTBALLERS.
THE RUGBY CODE.

J. MURRAY,
VICE-CAPTAIN, STOCKPORT R.F.C.

Before photos appeared in newspapers, drawings were the only illustrations

The original **Stockport Rugby Club** were founded in **1874** and played their first match that winter. In 1875, they were sharing a ground with another rugby team, Stockport Crusaders at Bramhall Lane - more than likely where Stockport Georgians now play. Their fixture list for season 1875-76 included the following teams: Manchester Grammar School, Stanley, Moss Side Wanderers, Greenheys, Fallowfield Rovers, Ashton-on-Mersey, Broughton 2nd, Chorlton, Pendleton and Cheadle. A match in January, 1875, Stockport were at Cheetham Hill v St. John's. Some of Stockport's players had made a mistake with the list of matches, so they fielded 13 to their opponents 16 but still won: Stockport 1 try, 1 disputed try, 1 touchdown, 1 rouge - St. John's 1 try, 1 touchdown (disputed), 1 rouge.

A report of a game in January, 1875:

### STOCKPORT v. STALYBRIDGE
**(1st Teams)**
**'This match was played on the Stalybridge ground on Saturday last, and resulted in a victory for the Stockport team by one try, two rouges, against three rouges for Stalybridge. The Stockport team**

**were overmatched both if weight and numbers, playing with only thirteen men to their opponents fifteen. The game commenced soon after three o'clock, the Stalybridge captain kicking off (down hill). The ball was kept for some time in the centre of the field, but owing to the superior numbers and strength of the Stalybridge team and the Stockportians were forced to touch the ball down three times in self defence before half time.**
**After changing ends Stockport played much better, and after twice compelling their opponents to touch down the ball, succeeded in scoring a try, which however was not converted in a goal, it being a very difficult kick. The Stockport team was composed of the following:- Mr. C. Bowlas (captain), Messrs. J. Green, H. Barlow, W. Wild, W. Ardern, W. Bowlas, G. Pearson, F. Collier, W. Gill, S. Potter, S. Royle, H. Pearson, J. Burtinshaw.'**

For the following season, the club had moved to a ground at Adswood Lane. As a result of an injury sustained in a home game v Grasshopper's Club (Manchester), a Stockport player died, the following Monday morning. Joseph Barlow, aged 21 from Greek Street, had been thrown over the shoulder of an opponent and caught on the side - complaining of 'great chest pain'. In view of this tragic death, the drastic action was taken to disband Stockport Rugby Club. As an alternative to Rugby, many of the players formed Stockport Lacrosse Club in 1876.

Stockport Rugby Club were reformed on September 30th 1881, when a practice match was played in a field off Adswood Lane West, according to the rules of the Sheffield Association. Maybe due to the tragic accident 5 years earlier, members of the club wanted to play the less fierce association game. This was only a temporary arrangement, as rugby soon took over again! Back in action for the 1881-82 season, early matches played in this campaign were against Cheadle Hulme and Higher Broughton clubs.

Prior to the 1887-88 season, railings were erected around the pitch to help control the fans, which now averaged around 1300. The highest crowd at the Adswood Lane ground was 3000, when they played Levenshulme. A shed was built as a wash-house for the players and the club adopted new colours of blue and white vertical stripes, shirts supplied by Samuel Barlow of Underbank. The excellent performance of the club for this season was: Played 28, Won 21, Lost 2, Drawn 5 - scoring 27 goals, 35 tries and 108 minors.

New land was purchased by Stockport Cricket Club in 1888 and resulted in an amalgamation with the rugby outfit and continued for 3 years at Cale Green.

During the whole of the time, there was not total harmony between the two sections, and in 1891 the Rugby Club moved to Edgeley Park - donated for sporting use by the Sykes family, owners of the Sykes Bleach Works. Within 2 years, there was a stand built, covering about 2/3rds down the reservoirs side of the ground plus a another small stand in the middle of what is now the 'open' railway end - they are shown on an ordnance survey map of 1893.

In the 1892-93 season, Stockport Rugby club was to play a match v Tuebrook. There was a large amount of hay around the ground in case of frost. Twenty minutes into the game, there was a blaze directly in front of the Press stand. 'A man with a pipe threw a match on the hay, fog around the ground was illuminated and allowed Stockport to drop a goal - the player used too much exertion and injured his knee cap'.

There were many rugby clubs in the North of England which wished to establish payment for bona fide lost working time to play the game. A meeting of the representatives of the Senior clubs of Lancashire and Yorkshire held a meeting at the 'George Hotel', Huddersfield in August, 1895 - to announce the formation of the Northern Rugby Football Union with 22 clubs as original members. Stockport was also included at the meeting at the 'George', after calling in by phone!

The first matches of the new Northern Union were played on September 7th, 1895. Stockport, known as the 'Clarets', opening game was v St. Helens in front of a crowd believed to be 10,000 - it must have been a tight fit at Edgeley Park! There were 2 competitions to be fought for - one for Lancashire (1st winners Runcorn) and one for the Yorkshire (Manningham Bradford) clubs plus leagues for the reserve teams.

In the same month as the start of the N.R.F.U., the Rugby Football Union made further by-laws to guard against professionalism and their clubs were forbidden to play North Union teams - it was a bitter severance of rugby into 2 rival camps! Over the following 8 years, RFU membership halved from 481 to 244 clubs as teams switched allegiance.

The Northern Union was a run-away success with 59 teams present at the first AGM and many more applications flooding in! The second season saw the introduction of a Challenge Cup, which all clubs were allowed to enter, causing great excitement, with the final at Headingley. From 1895 to 1908, the most significant changes to the rules were made and Rugby League was transformed into an entirely different game.

By the 1898-99 season, Stockport Rugby Club were starting to struggle in the Northern Union - finishing near to the bottom of the league.

## STOCKPORT RUGBY FOOTBALL CLUB

| Date | FIRST TEAM | Ground |
|------|------------|--------|
| **1899** | | |
| Sep. 2 | Altrincham | Home |
| " " 9 | Wigan | Home |
| " " 16 | Warrington | Away |
| " " 23 | Swinton | Home |
| " " 25 | Oldham | Home |
| " " 30 | Cumberland v Cheshire | (in Cumberland) |
| Oct 7 | Broughton Rangers | Home |
| " " 14 | Runcorn | Home |
| " " 17 | Oldham | Away |
| " " 21 | St. Helens | Away |
| " " 28 | Yorkshire v Cheshire | (in Cheshire) |
| Nov 4 | Warrington | Home |
| " " 11 | Rochdale Hornets | Away |
| " " 18 | Swinton | Away |
| " " 25 | St. Helens | Home |
| Dec 2 | Lancashire v Cheshire | (in Lancashire) |
| " " 9 | Broughton Rangers | Away |
| " " 16 | Runcorn | Away |
| " " 23 | Salford | Home |
| " " 25 | Millom (Cumberland) | Home |
| " " 30 | Widnes | Home |
| **1900** | | |
| Jan 1 | Millom | Away |
| " " 6 | Salford | Away |
| " " 13 | Leigh | Home |
| " " 20 | Tyldesley | Away |
| " " 27 | Rochdale Hornets | Home |
| Feb 3 | Morecambe | Home |
| " " 10 | Leigh | Away |
| " " 17 | Tydesley | Home |
| " " 24 | Widnes | Away |
| Mar 3 | Altrincham | Away |
| " " 10 | Wigan | Away |
| " " 17, 24, and 31, Cup-ties | | |
| Apr 7 and 14, Cup-ties | | |
| " " 16 | Morecambe | Away |

The Second X1 of Stockport Rugby Club played some of the Reserve teams as above, but in addition were matched with Lostock Gralam, Flixton, and Cadishead - vacant dates were filled up with friendly games.

The club had a pre-season friendly v Altrincham, including new players Beven, Gough, Williams and Trotter - winning by 16 points (2 goals, 4 tries) to Altrinchams' 0.

The first team captain was to be William Robinson - 'With the exception of Fred Saville probably no importation of the Stockport Rugby Club has done the first team greater service'.... 'One of the most dangerous wing three-quarters in a Lancashire Senior Competition'. He had been at the club for 3 years, joining from Heckmondwike (West Yorkshire) and now playing for his adopted County. William was still playing for Stockport, when the club folded and died in 1949 aged 75, living on Castle Street, Edgeley.

This never before published photo of Stockport Rugby Club playing at Edgeley Park c1895

Edgeley Park in the mid 1890s, the home of Stockport Rugby Club

During this season, the club reached the quarter-finals of the Cup Ties and bettered its position in the Competition table. However, there was some concern about the size of the gates at Edgeley Park - it was rare for the crowd to amount to 5000. Practically the whole of the 1899-1900 players were re-engaged for the next campaign, together with several really promising local youths.

There had been a Hazel Grove Rugby Club, the 'reds' were known as 'the poachers', but had folded earlier in the decade. This club had supplied Stockport with a number of players including Albert Garside, a forward of great renown - when in his prime, had few equals in Lancashire and Cheshire. James Taylor had also been recruited from Hazel Grove, 8 years earlier and soon impressed in the 'A' team and promoted into the first X1.

By today's standards, the majority of Rugby matches at this time were low scoring affairs. At least once a season there would be a 0-0 draw, i.e. when Stockport played Rochdale in season 1900-01. Stockport's poor record for this campaign was: Played 26 matches, won 6, 3 draws and 17 defeats - finishing 3rd from the bottom of the league with 15 points. Total receipts were £1,132 9s 3d, 1st team gates £685 7s, with an overall loss of £14 13s 7d.

For season 1901-02, Stockport had been severed from the top clubs in the Lancashire Section Competition, when the Northern League was installed, playing in the 2nd Division - a vastly inferior set of clubs.

There were various 'trial' matches before the start of season 1902-03: 'Reds' v 'Whites', 'Stripes' (1st team attack) v 'Reds' (1st team defence) and finally 'Probable' v 'Possibles'.

Stockport suffered their heaviest defeat since starting league rugby, going down 30-0 v Leeds at Headingly. Problems for an away game at Dewsbury; 'Stockport Rugby sent a short team to Dewsbury, a meeting of the League decided any case of a similar nature occurs the offender will be punished'. At the end of March the club had only gained 7 points in the Northern League.

Financial problems for the club were beginning to take their toll. Some of the players were not happy with 'money issues', and only 10 played in the fixture at Lancaster and finished the season bottom of the table.

Appearing in the *Cheshire Daily Echo* on August 1st 1903:

### STOCKPORT RUGBY FOOTBALL CLUB ANNUAL MEETING

**'The annual meeting of the members of the Stockport Rugby Club was held at the Commercial Hotel, Stockport, last evening. The meeting was private, only members being admitted. Contrary to custom, the representatives of the press were excluded. We are informed that the following business was transacted:-**

Stockport Rugby team pictured for season 1898-99

The balance sheet was presented, and it showed that in spite of the difficulties that had to be contended with last season, the committee had contrived to make ends meet. It was stated that debts amounting to about £70 were paid off, and but for this there would have been a problem upon last season's working.

The liabilities amounted to about £600.

The members of the committee, who acted last season, were re-appointed, and were empowered to decide what steps to take with regard to the forthcoming season.

The latter clause, we expect, refers to the question which has lately been so much discussed in Stockport, as to whether the club should be continued. We had previously been informed on good authority that terms relative to disband would be submitted to the members last evening, and though that statement has received official denial, it is expected that the club will shortly be disbanded. At any rate the exclusion of the Press from the annual meeting is very significant, as it points to the supposition that this question was under consideration'

FOOTNOTE: Having been in existence for 30 years, Stockport Rugby Club was sadly no more - after only one season sharing Edgeley Park, Stockport County now had the ground to themselves!

Cricket must have been played in the Hazel Grove area back to the middle of the 19th century. An early game in June 1870, was Hazel Grove Mechanics v Norbury - played on the ground of the former, for a ball presented by Mr. J. Charlton (Landlord of the 'Rising Sun'). The match resulted in a victory for the Hazel Grove team, which scored 93 to Norbury's 35. Another cricket game reported in the *Stockport Advertiser*, the following year - Hazel Grove Wesleyans v Stockport St. Marys.

In August 1879 (Wakes Week), a match was played on the ground near the 'Rising Sun' between 18 players from Hazel Grove & District and 11 of Stockport with 2 professionals. 'After a pleasant game the eleven scored an easy victory, doubling the score of their opponents'.

**Hazel Grove Cricket Club** can trace their beginnings back to the **1870s**. In 1872, there was a concert held to raise club funds at the Mechanics' Institution - the Hazel Grove Band and singers entertained before a supper.

There were not many cricket organisations around then, but the club was a member of the North Derbyshire League. Wakes (holiday) Monday was always a Gala Day, when Hazel Grove played Bollington - each team engaged a professional for the match. The Grove Silver Band was in attendance and all the people of the village seemed to be there - no one thought of going away on holiday until after the Wakes Monday cricket match!

In those days, the players used to hire horse-drawn wagonettes **(a 4-wheeled pleasure carriage of light construction, for 6 or 8 persons on seats facing each other, often with a removable cover, drawn by one or more horses)** for away games, usually from Sam Stubbs, who owned a horse with a very long neck which people called 'Stubby's giraffe'. Why you might ask? Because it was said, the horse held its head on one side so it could tell the time by the 'stores clock' every time she went past! Sometimes, Sam would lend the team the wagonette, provided they drove it themselves and bought the horse a feed. On one occasion, they forgot to give the horse its feed so, at the last place of call, the players pinched some sawdust out of the spitoon and just before handing the horse back to Sam, they rubbed the horse's nose in the sawdust to make believe it had been fed!

Hazel Grove Wesleyan Cricket Club was playing in September, 1898 on the grounds of a Mrs. Richardson of Norbury Moor.

In the 1880s, Hazel Grove played on a field behind the 'Rising Sun' alongside Macclesfield Road, now occupied by a carpet shop and bus terminus. September 1898 saw the last match staged on this ground - a new railway line connecting Cheadle Heath to New Mills was to be constructed, passing right through the cricket pitch! There was no cricket in 1899 and 1900, before a new site was found between the railway embankment and Norbury Churchyard, where they played until 1906. The first game on the new ground v Stockport 2nd X1, resulted in a win for the Stockport team by 5 wickets.

Clubs the 'Grove' played against then were: Hayfield, Strines, Marple, Birch Vale and Whaley Bridge. As was Poynton, who dismissed Hazel Grove at the Poynton Ground for 3 runs in 1905! Not surprisingly, the club disbanded in 1906, because of loss of players. Around this period, another team in Hazel Grove, known as the 'Rec' Team, who played on a dirt pitch on the Green Lane Recreation Ground, also folded.

In the same year, such players as John Marsland, Willie Ridgway and Ernest Hallworth joined some of the cricketers from the old Hazel Grove club and with players from the old 'Rec' club, they played as Hazel Grove Wesleyans. They were members of the Stockport & District League from 1907, with a ground at Old Fold Farm, Grosvenor Street, Hazel Grove. The club was given notice to quit the pitch and moved to Battersby Farm, Torkington Lane (now Hazelwood Road) - only one season there, as Lady Barlow complained about the wall in Torkington being damaged by spectators - so back to Grosvenor Street, an area behind what was then Wallers Mill, the same pavilion soon appeared on the ground!

This Stockport League consisted of 7 clubs in the Denton area, plus Reddish Vale and Heaton Norris - nearly every away game was at Denton! Hooley Hill

# Hazel Grove Cricket Club in 1883

Pictured in front of their pavilion, when the club played behind the 'Rising Sun' Inn are: Back row Sam Williamson, John Kellett, Billy Mitchell (Umpire), Martin Clough, Jack Fletcher, Sam Burns. Middle row George Hallam (Secretary), Anah Burns, Hobson, Sam Hallworth, Robert Penney. Front row Roberts, Jim Kellett, Higgonbotham

(Openshaw) was later admitted to the League and each club had its own umpire. The Wesleyans' first match v Hooley Hill started in controversy - the 'Grove' team put the opposition in and the first ball bowled, knocked back the stumps of the opening batsmen, but the umpire said 'NOT OUT', the reason being given 'it was a practice ball'!

During the years 1906-1911, the club didn't win any honours but faired well in the League. However, in 1912, Hazel Grove were joint Champions with Reddish Vale and played off at Heaton Norris Cricket Ground, Green Lane, where they lost by 2 wickets. Opening batsman, Walter Taylor was hit on the head by a throw-in and took no further part - he was the 'star' player, and it was felt that this incident lost them the match! Everything was put right next season - the Wesleyans winning the League. Buxworth and Bredbury were admitted, because 2 of the Denton Clubs dropped out.

In a match v Aspinall (near Denton), the Hazel Grove side were dismissed for 21 runs - the opposition were all out for a total of only 9 runs, with the remarkable feat of John Daniels and Charlie Thorpe, both achieving a hat-trick! 'Jackson's', the outfitters in Princess Street, Stockport stated 'if they were presented with a form signed by the League Secretary, they would donate the lucky bowlers with bowler hats'! These 2 bowlers went through the season taking 89 wickets at just over 3 runs per wicket!

The match away to Buxworth, was considered to be an annual picnic outing, with a wagonette hired by the Wesleyans from the Stockport Carriage Company. The coach was carried by a team of 3 horses and set off from Hazel Grove, conveying the cricketers and supporters. At Bridgemont, all the occupants had to get off, because the road was dangerous - later they all were back inside to continue the trip to Buxworth, paying the required toll at the Toll Bar between the 2 villages. Tea had been arranged for a party of about 30 at the 'Navigation Inn', the landlady of which used to live in the 'Grove'.

The Wesleyans won the toss, batted and scored 130 - a high score as 50 was considered good! After this innings, the 'Grove' ladies went off to the Inn to make teas, but before they could get started, one of them announced "th'chaps are comin' off th' field, what's up! "We've won", it was shouted by one of the cricketers. Buxworth, having been all out for just 13, Charlie Thorne again earning himself another bowler hat!

At the end of each season, Hazel Grove did not have sufficient cash to pay the rent (£3 per annum) to the farmer, and he had to be asked for an extension of time in which to pay! On one occasion, on the Friday night, it was found that one of the bats was broken (they only had 2). The club had no money, so one of the players (Billy Spencer) lent them £2 so as to be able to buy a bat the following morning for the afternoon match!

Season 1914 was again a successful one , but the Wesleyans lost the Championship on the last day of the season, being beaten by Bredbury St. Marks.

It was at this point, that the Wesleyan Chapel Recreation Society was looking for a field large enough for cricket, football and tennis - a site at Haigh's Farm was suitable. So Hazel Grove Wesleyan CC returned to the old ground, which was rented for £20 per annum. The cricket section quickly got to work and laid another playing pitch for £10, and the pavilion once again re-appeared!

The 1914-18 Great War now intervened, just as the Society appeared to be getting prosperous. By the end of 1915, with so many players in the Army, it was realised that all organised out-door sports were impossible - the tenancy had to be given up.

In 1873, Compstall Athletic Club arranged a competition starting from the 'Hare and Hounds'. To be run several miles over Ludworth Moor, Cown's Rocks and Mottram with Werneth Low. A paper trail was laid 2 hours before the start - there were 10 entries but only 7 athletes took part. The winner was Tom Vaughan from Manchester, who finished at 6pm - the last runners finished in the dark! Prizes were awarded at the 'Horse Shoe Inn', Marple Bridge by Williams Gilmore, who entered, but arrived too late to run.

Mellor Stag Hunt from the preserves of the Earl of Stamford and Warrington, starting a meeting from the 'Lamb Inn', Rowarth. 'Fine sport was brought to Strines, a large number of sportsmen joined the chase'.

A Billiard match was arranged between Edgeley v Heaton Norris Conservative Newsrooms. Twelve players each side took part - Edgeley scored 500, Heaton Norris 504. Billiards was also taking place at Stockport Reform Club, 6 members in a contest v Glossop Liberal Club - the former being victors 509 to 503.

By 1875, 2 Rugby clubs of some note in the town were the Stockport Wellington Club, who played at Adswood and Stockport Crusaders, based at Bramhall Lane. These 2 outfits had similar fixture lists to Stockport Rugby Club. There were reports on other clubs i.e. Birch, Rovers, Zingari, Greenheys, but no way of knowing where they were located!

Whilst there were one or two private bowling clubs, the vast majority of bowling was taking place on an Inn's bowling green. For the second time, there was an All England Bowling match in the area - held on this occasion at the Windsor Castle, Edgeley. Sixty four players fought for a first prize of £5, donated by the landlord - the entrance money was divided for other prizes. The action started at 1pm, but after 3 rounds, it was too dark , the match was finished the following day.

There was the Victoria Club on Hall Street, who were up against the strong Stockport CC team in 1876, Scores: Doubles - Stockport 78, Victoria 58. Singles - Stockport 129, Victoria 75. The former won by 74.

**Compstall Cricket Club** were formed in the **1870's** - prior to this there had been various cricket clubs in this small village. They were Compstall Bridge, who were playing at Stockport Improvement (Cheadle Heath) in 1865. Royal George, a game in 1868 was a 'local derby' away at Strines - during the match the Strines Brass Band were in evidence! Other clubs were Compstall Improvement and Compstall United. Where 3 of the teams played remains a mystery, but the Royal George played its matches on the land behind the present 'George Hotel', before reforming as Compstall Cricket Club and moving to the present ground on Ernocroft Road. In 1872, 120 members of the Royal George held their opening dinner and ball at the Athenaeum (public reading room) in Compstall - plenty of loyal toasts and dancing took place!

There is a report of a Compstall game in 1875, when they hammered New Mills, scores Compstall 104, New Mills 14! Sometimes, the newspapers didn't show the full title of a club, so it is difficult to tell if a new Compstall team had now started.

Many of these early games were apparently accompanied by the sounds of the Compstall Band, and as many as 150 would take tea to meet and listen to the band plus watch cricket. In the 1890s, Compstall played in the North Derbyshire & Stockport District League - later taking part in the Glossop & District League against fellow members such as Hadfield, Hazel Grove, Hayfield, New Mills, Chapel-en-le-Frith, Bredbury and Romiley.

**Stockport Lacrosse Club is the oldest surviving club in England, being founded in 1876.** Sometime early in 1876, a group of rugby players were travelling from Manchester's London Road station to Stockport on their way home from a match in which a team member had been seriously injured. From the carriage window, whilst the train had stopped at a signal, they saw the spectacle of a running game with players waving strange sticks around their heads and encircled by a large crowd. The seed was sown at this moment and soon after lacrosse was established in Stockport.

The players were members of Stockport Rugby Club which was to be, or had just been, disbanded due to a fatal accident. Whatever the size or actual spectacle of the lacrosse game they saw, its impact was such that it inspired the formation of the club for a sport that had hardly been seen before.

The Lacrosse match being played that day along side the railway at Longsight Cricket Club (now built on)

was between the teams of the Canadian Montreal Club and Caughnawaga Indians. Their tour to this country took place in April 1876 and was part of a revival occurring in Southern England. The 2 teams had received an invitation from a Dr. T. Archer, who played in Montreal, but in 1876 was in Wimbledon and having formed a club there, wished to promote the growth of lacrosse in England.

Exhibition games were played in Birmingham, Belfast, Dublin, Edinburgh, Newcastle and Sheffield as well as Manchester. The 'Illustrated London News' reported that lacrosse was 'received with the greatest favour' and recommended it as an 'antidote to football' which was considered too rough!

The Stockport Club was the sixth to be formed, those earlier being: London, Manchester, Sheffield, Blackheath (London) and Broughton (Salford). Manchester played at Old Trafford Cricket Ground and Broughton at Broughton Cricket Ground - all these clubs have now ceased to exist.

The inaugural meeting of Stockport Lacrosse Club took place at the house of Dr. Massey in Greek Street, Stockport. Their ground for the first few seasons was a field where Lowfield Road joins Shaw Heath, now built over by Beaconsfield Villa.

The earliest game for which records exist was on March 17th 1877 v Broughton, played at Stockport Cricket Club - the result being 5-0 to the visitors. The early playing years were not very successful - Stockport were not able to beat any of the first clubs to be formed and even struggled against later outfits such as Chorlton, Heaton Mersey, Cheetham and Cheadle. The Jubilee booklet records: 'that in one season the only match won was the very last one of the season'. In the early 1880s, the club moved grounds to join Stockport Cricket Club, which then played at Charles Street , Higher Hillgate. At the AGM in November, 1883, Stockport Lacrosse Club was invited by the cricket club to pay rent for the first time and join them at Cale Green for the winter season.

Around this time seemed to be the turning point and the Stockport players began to win matches - in November 1881, the clubs 3 teams in existence, all won their games with a total of 30 goals against 3! 1st beat Widnes 15-1, A beat Withington B 12-0 and B beat Fairfield Wells A 3-2.

Playing standards however, had not sufficiently risen in time for the first season of the Senior Flags competition in 1883-84, losing 2-1 to Heaton Mersey in the first round. It was not until 1895-96, that a semi-final place was reached v Cheetham, played on the Didsbury ground. At full time, the score was level and an extra 30 minutes was played in which Stockport took and held a 1 goal lead to qualify for the final for the first time.

Stockport Lacrosse at Crystal Palace 1895-96

Stockport (Northern Flag winners) v Southern Flag victors. The F.A. Cup Finals 1895-1914 were played at the Crystal Palace ground

The Cheshire team pictured in front of Stockport CC pavilion in 1904 v Canada

The Canadian team posing before the match v Cheshire

The opponents in the final were the 7 time winners, South Manchester but their hopes for an 8th victory was dashed as Stockport were victorious by 9-5. This first Senior Flags win of 1896, was the start of 2 all conquering periods - for **8 consecutive seasons until 1903, Stockport swept aside all opposition to win the Flags, a record that has not been equalled!** In the same period, the Iroquois Cup and First Division Championship were both won six times!

The club has to thank in particular 2 families, the Mason's and the Johnson's, whose family members made up between them 9 out of the total of 20 who played in the team!

A major trophy of the period remains in the possession of the club - this is the Flags Final Challenge Flag, which was won outright in 1898.

The close of the 1902-03 season saw the beginning of the retirement of some of the best players of the previous decade and the introduction policy of rebuilding.

Visiting teams like Toronto in 1902 and Ottawa in 1907 helped to improve the standard of play, plus the participation of lacrosse in the 1908 Olympic Games in London. The playing skills learnt were accurate and hard passing movements and judicious dodging, and when used in a more direct line to goal, proved to be an effective style of play.

There were many clashes with South Manchester of which the 1906-07 Flags Final was considered the toughest and was won by the opposition by 3-2. Such was the determination of both teams that it went to 2 extra periods - amounting to a total playing time of 2 hours! The consensus of the lacrosse administrators was that match periods of this length were far too long, and for future seasons should a draw occur, then a replay would take place.

In 1907, the Capitol Club of Canada toured England, defeating various All-England combination sides except for a draw in their final game v the Stockport Club. Emanuel Tasse, President of the Canadian team, led the tour with a squad that was recognised on both sides of the Atlantic as being a 'professional World Champion side'. 'The Cap's' declared Stockport's Gerald Mason to be 'the best player at Point on both sides of the Atlantic', following his performance in the England game in London and Stockport at Cale Green.

The Capital's game v Stockport was not part of the original tour itinerary and created a degree of animosity when proposals were made to arrange a game in advance of their arrival in England. At Stockport's committee meeting in March 1907, held at the 'Blossoms Hotel', it was resolved to 'apply to the agent of the Canadians to arrange a match and offer them one half of the gross gate receipts.'

By no means an insubstantial offer given that spectator attendances could be expected to be around 3-4000. The agents reply considered it 'too little as 75% was the amount usually offered, and that he had laid the whole matter before Mr. Tasse'. The final outcome of the 'financial' deal was not recorded in the minutes!

During the 1907-08 season, the Cheshire clubs were in protest with the North of England Lacrosse Association (NELA) regarding a new bye-law which placed the Cheshire Lacrosse Association in a subordinate role. A Stockport member wished to donate a cup for a competition for any club in Cheshire and was known as the Stockport Cup - the cup to be insured by the winning club for £20. No breakaway by Cheshire or their clubs occurred.

A Stockport and District team was assembled for the match, which included no less than 8 Stockport players. A crowd of 3,000 saw a 'never to be forgotten game' end in a 4-4 draw.

The second of the 'all conquering' periods commenced in 1910 and spanned 3 seasons until 1913 - during which the Iroquois and Flags were won each year and the League twice.

The 1912 Flags Final was won 7-3 v Albert Park, and the following season provided a re-match which was won 15-2! The resulting Iroquois Cup match, to become Champions of England was won 22-4 v Lee for the 3rd year in succession.

Eighty-seven of the club's total membership of 160, gave their services to King and Country in the 'Great War' of 1914-18. The names of all these members are recorded on the Roll of Honour Memorial Tablet erected to their memory, and it is still there at the club's headquarters.

In 1878 there was a report of a bowling match at the 'Royal Oak', Commercial Road, Hazel Grove. Twelve men of Hazel Grove v 12 men of Marple - the 'Grove' scored 124 points to Marple's 66.

Cricket clubs were continuing to 'spring up' all over the Stockport area, some more appearing in the press for the first time: Offerton, Handforth, Edgeley University, Flowery Field, Wellington Road United, Heaton Moor, Wilmslow, Stockport Great Moor, Stepping Hill, Hillgate Victory, Heaton Norris Wanderers, Portwood True Blues, St. Mathew's United and Hempshaw Lane Victoria.

There was temporarily little mention of Rugby, one local club, Heaton Mersey Ramblers (1 touchdown) v Cavendish ( 3 goals, 1 try, 2 touchdowns). When 16 men of Heaton Moor (1 try disputed, 2 touchdowns, 1 dead ball) played Eccles 2nd team 0, for the first time the size of the crowd was shown, 300 people.

7000 Crowd Watch Lacrosse at Cale Green

The Cheshire v Canada game in progress, part of the large crowd lining the touchlines can be seen

Marple had introduced a rugby team, but somewhat struggled at first: In a 14 a side match, Newton Heath (1 poster, 6 tries, 5 touchdowns), Marple 0. Manchester Rovers 15 players (2 goals, 7 tries, 2 touchdowns) Marple 0. In many of the early sporting encounters, it was often difficult to know the strength of the opposition, resulting in 'one-sided' matches.

Billiards was a winter sport becoming more popular in the town - 8 players of the Stockport Conservative Association (660 points) v Edgeley Conservative Club (739).

In 1879, Heaton Moor and Heaton Mersey were semi-rural suburbs of Stockport - fields separated the fine new villas and the old cottage property from Manchester's growing sprawl, and industry creeping along the Mersey valley out of Stockport. They were pleasant districts, appreciated by early commuting businessmen and growing in popularity for their social desirability. Social life in the Heatons was centred upon Heaton Moor Reform Club and the churches, and Manchester and Stockport were within easy reach for the occasional theatre or concert.

Everyday requirements could be bought at the local shops, but Victorian housewives looked forward to their shopping trips 'in town' to replenish wardrobes or furnishings.
Farmland surrounded the 2 areas, and it was on one of these farm fields that a Cricket and Lacrosse Club had its first home.

Heaton Mersey Sunday School was the first cricket club of any stature, their first reported game was in 1861 v Clayton (Manchester) - winning by 12 runs on the Clayton ground.

**Heaton Mersey Cricket and Lacrosse Club** was founded in **1879**, at a meeting of 5 local men held at the Church School Committee Room on October 16th. A leather-backed exercise book which contains the record of the meeting shows several basic decisions were taken. The name of the new club was established, and it was to rent a field (with a considerable slope) comprising 3 acres, next to the South side of Didsbury Road, near to Bank Hall - only a field away from where Heaton Norris Rovers (Stockport County) played in 1885-86 at Underbank Farm.

There had been an earlier Heaton Mersey Cricket Club, which had been playing for several seasons earlier in the decade i.e. in 1874 they were in a match v Charlestown, one of the better clubs in the Stockport area. Later that summer, there was a report of their match being played at Burnage v Macclesfield.

John McClure was elected President, R. Le Mare Junior the Secretary and Frank Yates became Treasurer. The committee was to consist of the officers and Messrs. F. Menzies, F. Knowler, G. Webb, W. Broughton and A. Jackson. There were 17 playing members nominated for membership and accepted.

Arrangements were soon made to put the ground in order, and social activities were planned to raise funds to provide a pavilion and to finance the club's activities. Fixing the subscription at one guinea, the committee 'agreed to take sole responsibility for the first year in money matters, and will not have power to call upon any member for more than his subscription'.

The club jersey colours of navy blue with inch-wide stripes were chosen, and 'the field let to R. Crompton at 10/- (50p) per month, half an acre to be mown by us if we require it'.

Rules were drawn up, approved and printed and permission was given to the secretary to arrange 2 matches with Stretford Lacrosse Club on each others grounds - the first game played December 20th, 1879. The first season's lacrosse fixture list included matches v Bramhall, Stockport, Cheadle, Didsbury, Stretford and Chorlton.

The turn of 1879 saw the committee seeking estimates for a pavilion, and organising a cricket season and also a lawn tennis club. F. Knowler was appointed Cricket Captain, and in May the committee minuted 'that two bats be bought for the use of the club, one at 9/6d. and one at 11/6d.

The subscription to the lawn tennis section was to be 5/- (25p) per annum. Two tennis nets with poles were ordered costing 21/- per set, also one pair of racquets at 6/6d., and one dozen tennis balls. The racquets were for the use of visiting friends. The rule was passed 'that no member of the Club be allowed to play without wearing shoes with India rubber soles, or shoes without heels'.

At the first AGM of the Heaton Mersey Cricket and Lacrosse Club in October 1880, the rules of the North of England Lacrosse Association were accepted, and delegates elected. Although tennis was played, it was not formally incorporated in the title of the Club until 1907.

Increased club activities called for more financial resources, and December 1880, saw the first of many concerts to raise funds. These were held in St. John's Church schoolrooms, and tickets cost 2/- (10p) and 1/-.
Early in 1881, an additional piece of land was laid for cricket practice, and by April the club had engaged a Grounds-man at the princely sum of 5/- per week.

The question of a new pavilion was discussed and plans were put before the March meeting of 1882. One estimate of £202 was received. Someone heard of a second-hand pavilion for sale at Macclesfield - offering £20, but the deal fell through! However, an estimate from W. & T. Meadows at £149 was accepted. This pavilion can be seen on an ordnance survey map.

At the end of the lacrosse season, a match was arranged v Cambridge University, and an entrance fee of 6d. was given to the pavilion fund. An important step for the tennis section - a 'cinder tennis court' was laid in one corner of the field.

The minutes from 1883 state -'It was resolved that E. Oldham having used the cricket field for an unauthorised cricket match, and also wilfully broken a tennis pole, the property of the club, he be charged 10/6d. For the use of the field, and 9d., the net cost of the tennis pole, and that he be reprimanded by the secretary!'

In season 1883-84, Heaton Mersey Lacrosse reached the first final of the Senior Flags competition - losing 8-5 v South Manchester.

At the fourth annual meeting in 1883, there were now 58 playing members. The pavilion finally cost £170, the field had been re-fenced with iron rails on 2 sides, and the club fielding 2 lacrosse and 2 cricket teams. By now cricketers were being paid and the possibility of engaging a professional was considered, £30 for the season. Eventually, F. Watson of Stockport was signed up for the first 12 weeks of the season of 1884, at the weekly wage of 30/- (£1.50). For the first time, a horse was purchased for £4 to pull the roller at the beginning of the season.

By 1888, with over 100 members, the club fielded 3 lacrosse teams, and the Top Field, Heaton Mersey, was rented at £2 for the season for the use of the third team. During the years 1888-93, J.F.B. Adam brought honour to the club as he represented England, Lancashire and the North.

In June 1890, came a major blow - the landlord Mr. J. Albiston, gave the club 6 months notice to quit, as the land was to be used for development. It was not until December 1891, that an arrangement was made with a Mr. Bardsley for the tenancy of a 5 acre plot near Clifton Road and Green Lane, Heaton Moor - a sum of £300 had to be raised! Life membership was offered at 10 guineas to acquire some ready cash!

Whilst the Clifton Road was considered, the decision was made to take the Green Lane ground on a lease of not less than 3 years, with the option of purchase. All in all £2,228 would be required to complete the transfer, and nearly £416 had already been promised. A tennis pavilion was bought for £15 from Reddish Lawn Tennis Club - someone donated 1,000 square yard of turf - a neighbour offered to supply the club with hot water for tea on the opening day.

The new cricket ground was opened by the President, Mr. Joseph Leigh J.P. in May 1893.

The A.G.M. of 1895, heard that 2 new cricket pitches had been laid and 3 tennis courts designed to run parallel with each other. The option to buy the land at

£1,978 was taken up - a huge bazaar which ran for 4 days, raised £1,835.

The district the club served in 1900 was still mainly rural, with a large number of farms and several large family estates. The remainder of the population was mostly upper middle class, living in large houses. It is not difficult to imagine that the Heaton Mersey Club was a genteel establishment, recognising the social graces, and markedly class conscious! It was reported that certain members played cricket on Sunday, and it was hoped would never occur again!

A Ladies' Hockey Section had also be added to the list of sports, making a total club membership of 282 - 43 life members, 141 full members, 41 lacrosse and 57 tennis and hockey.

From 1902, the beginning of each cricket season was marked by employing a professional or a grounds man. The 1903 minutes refer to engaging 'a ground bowler and umpire (or to play if necessary), at 15/- (75p) per week.

By 1907, so many lady members wanted to play tennis, that the committee feared congestion on the courts!

Croquet, too was popular and applications were received for membership of a new section.

In 1910, the hockey section nearly folded and only continued after a revised subscription rate was fixed! It was stipulated that only tennis members were to be eligible for election to play hockey.

The year 1911 saw the cricket section expand to include a section for under-18's. The lacrosse team reached third place in the league table, their highest ever except for the 1904-5 season, and reached the semi-final in the Senior Flags competition.

Staffing trouble came to a head this year, when the committee found the grounds man, F. Taylor, shirking his duties regarding the practice wickets, and in no uncertain terms he was threatened with instant dismissal without notice if he did not mend his ways!

In September, 1913, the opportunity was taken at a club event at the Reform Club to present the chairman, Robert Crook, with a magnificent Chippendale design 8-day grandfather clock as appreciation for 21 years' service.

The new clock's chimes rang in the end of an era, not only for the chairman but for the club too, as the dark clouds of war gathered on the horizon. Heaton Mersey Cricket, Tennis and Lacrosse Club was never to recapture the atmosphere of those pre-First World War years.

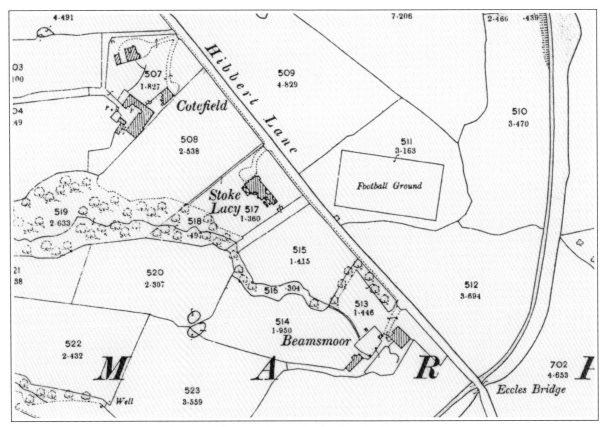

The ground where Marple F.C. played is shown in this 1890s map

There was still no local association football games reported in either of the 2 Stockport newspapers in the late 1870s, although by now the 'round ball' will have been played. A rare feature was the annual match Lancashire v Cheshire in March 1879 at Turton (the first football club in Lancashire). A crowd of 1,400 saw the Lancashire team win easily 6-2. The Cheshire side were made up by players from: Macclesfield, Crewe, Northwich and Chester College. The officials consisted of 2 umpires and a referee.

**The first reference to Lacrosse was in February, 1880:** Cheadle Cricket & Lacrosse Club 0 v Heaton Mersey 3 (1 disputed) - Didsbury 0 v Blackley 3 - Stockport 0 v Broughton 3.

**Local Association Football appeared in the press for the first time in October 1880,** although still not in Stockport but popular in Macclesfield. The first game included was Rainow v Macclesfield 2nd Team, on the ground of the former - Macclesfield winning 2-1. Other matches were: St. Georges Rangers 1 v Macclesfield 0, played at Sutton Hall. Rainow 2nd Team 3 v Bollington White Star 0, played at the Shrigley Vale ground. Messrs Brocklehurst Employees (Macclesfield) 3 v Chester Road 2.

By November 1881, Football & Rugby reports were placed together under a general heading of 'FOOTBALL'. Macclesfield matches still shown: Silver Medal Competition 1st Round, Baptist Rangers 3 v Chester Road Recreation 0, played at Sutton Hall.

Bollington 2 v Buxton 1 (the first time the 2 teams had played each other), Langley Rovers 2 v Leek 0.

**Cheadle Hulme Cricket Club** was founded in **1881.** The club was originally located next to Ladybridge (Leathers) Farm, Ladybridge Road. Many years later, moving to their present ground at Grove Park, on the other side of the village.

By 1895, the club had progressed to a high enough life to enable the *Stockport Advertiser* to write thus: 'There is perhaps no cricket club in the Manchester and District which has made more progress in the last few seasons than the Cheadle Hulme organisation. Cheadle Hulme now playing Manchester, Sale, Rusholme, Longsight - the club has risen to the top rank as regards Cheshire cricket'. By 1897, the club had staged their 8th match v the prestigious Stockport team - on this occasion scoring 49 to Stockport's 169.

In 1882, Cheshire played their annual football match v Staffordshire, on this occasion at Macclesfield. - the previous game had ended in a draw at Stoke. Three of the Cheshire players failed to turn up, resulting in 3 'substitute' members of the Macclesfield team being drafted in! A large crowd witnessed the Staffs team defeat Cheshire by 4-1.

By the 1880s, scoring points by the 'Rouge' method in Rugby were no longer featured. Scoring was still some way from today's rules, e.g. when Stockport Rugby

# The Birthplace of Stockport County F.C.

McLaughlin's Coffee House, Heaton Lane, where several Stockport youths met in 1883 to form Heaton Norris Rovers

45

Club played Cheadle Hulme in 1882, the scoring was: Stockport 1 goal, 5 touchdowns, 2 touch in goals, 2 dead balls. Cheadle Hulme 1 try, 1 touchdown. The main clubs competing were: Stockport, Cheadle, Cheadle Hulme, Heaton Mersey, Stockport Rangers and Marple. Cheadle advertised their home games in the press:

**CHEADLE FOOTBALL CLUB**
**v SWINTON**
**Dressing Rooms George & Dragon Hotel**
**NEW GROUND, WILMSLOW ROAD, CHEADLE**
**Admission 3d Ladies Free**
**Kick off 3.30**

Rugby was initially established in Marple but not long afterwards, the **Marple Football Club** had been founded c. **1882** and was to become a significant association team in the Stockport area. The majority of the team were local mill workers. Their ground was located on the Marple village side next to Hibbert Lane, with a considerable slope - now covered by Sherwood Close, Goyt Road and Barlow Crescent, Greenbank Crescent and Brook Drive.

In 1886, Marple played in a prestige match v Manchester at Hullard Hall Lane, Old Trafford, losing by 2-1. In the return game at Marple, the home side lost by 3-0. In 1888-89, Marple travelled to play Heaton Norris Rovers (Stockport County), winning by 3-1 with only 10 men - one of the first clubs to play at the Rovers then new ground at Green Lane.

By the 1892-93 season, the stature of the Marple club had risen to the level of playing Chester in the Cheshire Senior Cup. Before a crowd of 1000, Marple fought back from 4-1 down, to lose by 4-3. No doubt due to the decline in the textile industry and less players available, the club was in decline before the turn of the century. A later club, Marple Amateurs, were playing in the Stockport & District League in season 1911-12. The following season, the 'Amateurs' won the Cheshire Amateur Cup Final at Chester v Harrowby - 'a large number of Marple supporters went to Chester'.

For season 1914-15, Marple were to join the South East Lancashire League. The club's headquarters were the 'Pineapple Hotel'. The balance sheet showed a profit of 2s 6d, £5 rent was paid for their ground and the trainer's requisites amounted to 7s 6d.

By 1883, Lacrosse was continuing to become popular - some of the clubs in the area: Cheadle, Heaton Mersey Ramblers, Didsbury, Stockport, Reddish and Heaton Mersey. There was a prestige match for the Heaton Mersey club, when this year they entertained Cambridge University, losing by 4-2 before a good sized crowd. Another big game to take place was Lancashire v Cheshire, played at Longsight Cricket Club - the proceeds to go to Warehousemen & Clerks School, Cheadle Hulme.

To find the origins of **Stockport County Football Club,** we have to travel back to the summer of **1883,** to an establishment locally known as 'McLaughlin's Café'. For many years, the site of this café was thought to have been near to what is now Hooper Street and where the 'Classic' Cinema once stood on Wellington Road South. William McLaughlin did own the premises at no. 19, which were described as 'dining rooms', but the business did not open until 1893! In 1895 it is listed as the 'Station Coffee House' with commercial accommodation - a year later it became a Temperance (no alcohol) Hotel at numbers 15-17-19.

Stockport Sunday School, where County's founders were educated

**The correct location where the meeting of several youths was held to form Heaton Norris Rovers was in a Coffee House at 81, Heaton Lane.** In 1883, Heaton Lane extended on both sides of Wellington Road - the site is now open, on the corner of Princess Street (re-named after Royal visit) and Wellington Road South - directly opposite both the 'George' and 'Debenhams' - now a bus 'drive through'. William McLaughlin also owned this Café with 'rooms' - the tobacconists at no. 77, were owned by Peter Walters, who became one of the original directors of the club, when it became a limited company in 1908. There was a plan to establish 'superior' Coffee Houses in conjunction with Temperance Hotels, providing Billiards, Chess and other games, together with non-intoxicating drinks - hoping to be popular with young men of the town.

Maybe the all important meeting was on a Sunday, when they would have all been together for Sunday School. In an interview with the *Stockport Advertiser* in 1950, **WILLIAM RIDGWAY** stated: 'The first team was connected in the main with Wycliffe Sunday School. The other ten players were: **TOM MACHIN, TED WHITTLE, STAN HOCKENHILL, TOM RICHARDS,** the brothers **BROADBENT, SAMUEL** and **WILLIAM RILEY, TED SIMPSON** and **JACK HEWITT. BEN KELLY** joined the team shortly afterwards'.

William Ridgway, wearing a 'bowler hat' badge in the old County colours of red & white

The boys were aged 14 to 17 and lived in different central areas of the town. They would have known each other from their time spent at Stockport Sunday School, Wellington Street and also attending the Sunday School (long since demolished) at Wycliffe Congregational Church, Wellington Road North, Heaton Norris. Pupils at Stockport S.S. were taken to various places of worship in Stockport - Wycliffe was one of 9 such churches.

Many people, little more than children, worked in the numerous mills in Stockport town centre from a very young age. Most of these young men would have been working during the week, but attended Stockport Sunday School for their education on a Sunday morning from 9am-12pm. In addition some would also go to night school at Stockport SS, to help them to learn a trade and introduce the youths to sport - most importantly football! Their visits to the Sunday School at Wycliffe Church would have been more of a religious nature, but also still involved sport.

The Stockport Sunday School register, shows that Samuel Riley attended in 1881and 1882 in 8th Class Division 1. He was born in 1869, making him the youngest of the founder members at only 14!

Whilst Tom Machin, Ben Kelly and Ted Whittle all lived until 1950, the last to leave us was William Ridgway in 1961. On the occasion of his 90th birthday in 1956, he was visited by a *Stockport Advertiser* reporter, and his parting remark was: "Come and see me again when I'm 100" - he didn't make it to 100 but the ripe old age of 95! He was then living on Grimshaw Street, Stockport, the same street as one of his brothers. There were 24 birthday cards and a greetings telegram from his 21 year old grandson. "I'm the only one left of the lads who founded the present Stockport County Football Club", he told the reporter. His daughter, Mrs. Hannah Duckworth, made a birthday cake on which in blue icing against a white background was written '1866-1956. Still going strong'.

William Ridgeway (17 in 1883), a retired boiler fireman, was born in Portwood. At the age of 11 he was 'half-timing' (a child attending school for half-time and engaged in some occupation the rest of the day) in a local cotton mill - "Laying bobbins on at 2s. 6d. a week", he recalled. Like many of his friends, he was a keen footballer - playing both at right-half and in goal. When the club was still at Green Lane, Mr. Ridgway stated "I left them then and helped to form the Stockport and District League". William Ridgway is mentioned as being on the committee of the Stockport League at their AGM in November 1893.

Tom Machin

Tom Machin was aged 16, when he started playing in goal and full-back for Heaton Norris Rovers, when the club first starting playing on Heaton Norris Recreation Ground. In 1937, together with Messrs Kelly and Whittle, they were made life members of Stockport County. He was also a life member of Stockport Cricket Club.

As a young man, Mr. Machin started in business as a cycle dealer in Wellington Road South - being one of the first such dealers in Stockport. He was a keen cyclist and took part in races. He was one of the earliest members of Stockport Golf Club, and a member of Davenport Golf Club. In 1902, he built Shaw Heath Laundry and was connected with it for the rest of his working life. He did not retire until 1948, his only son, Councillor Clifford Machin taking over the business. Tom Machin of Davenport Park Road, died in 1950 aged 83 - his son was touring the French Alps by car and sadly couldn't make it to the funeral.

Ted Whittle was 17, when Heaton Norris Rovers started. He was born in Portwood (as William Ridgway) and started his working life as a hatter at Royle's in Adswood. When his playing days were over, Ted became a league linesman and later for 20 years in charge of the 'gate' at Edgeley Park. In 1900 he took the grocer's shop at Adswood Road East, where he died aged 84. He was an active bowler and won the Jarvis Cup at Stockport Cricket Club when he was almost 70!

Ben Kelly

Ben Kelly aged 15 (1883), died in his 82nd year, also in 1950, at the Nottingham home of his youngest daughter - having left his previous residence in Garners Lane, a few months earlier. In 1948, he said of modern football: 'The rising spiral of transfer fees is no good for the game .... I'm sorry good fair shoulder charging is going out'!

For 47 years Ben was with the Stockport firm of Hanson & Scott, rope and twine makers. He was prominently connected with St. Mark's Church. Ben Kelly had been a sides-man (assistant churchwarden) and for many years was treasurer of the annual rose fete which raised many hundreds of pounds for the church.

In the summer of 1882, William Ridgway and Ben Kelly were playing cricket for the Church team, under the name of Wycliffe Sunday School Band of Hope. The following season of 1883, there were sufficient members of the Sunday School to field a 2nd XI. The Wycliffe Cricket team were struggling: St. Paul's Brinnington 32, Wycliffe 17 & 12. New Zealand Victory 40, Wycliffe 17 (played at Major Turner's grounds, 'Woodlands', Offerton). However, later in the summer, victories followed - Openshaw 29, Wycliffe 39. Hanover Albion 75, Wycliffe 95. A scorecard from July, 1883:

**WYCLIFFE SUNDAY SCHOOL (1st Eleven) v. HEAVILEY IMPROVEMENT**

On the ground of the latter.

Score:- **Wycliffe Sunday School:**
**S. Riley** c Brown b H Hazeldine 4
**J. Holden** b L Smith 10
F. Wilkinson c Hazeldine b H Hazeldine 10
J. Baker c Hazeldine b L Smith 0
W. Williams c Downs b L Smith 1
**J. Hewitt** b H Hazeldine 0
**W. Ashworth** b L Smith 6
**W. Ridgway** b Hazeldine 4
J. Bristol b Hazeldine 2
A. Shottin not out 6
J. Higgins c Brown b L Smith 4
Extras 5 Total 52
**Heaviley Improvement** Total 30

**\* Players in bold were either founder members of Stockport County, or later played for Heaton Norris Rovers.**

There is evidence also of a football section in existence, so we ask the question why did these young men want to form their own team? They would now have been almost too old to continue at Wycliffe Sunday School, and would have wanted their independence. The teenagers would have noticed that other Association teams were starting up in Stockport. Several other League clubs owe their existence to Sunday School teams i.e. Bolton Wanderers, Everton and Fulham.

Whatever the founders' reasons, the new club they called Heaton Norris Rovers didn't initially totally break away as their first ground was the Heaton Norris Recreation Ground, where the Sunday school teams were already playing. The Council had purchased this land for recreation purposes in 1871 - a cricket team called Heaton Norris Recreation Ground (sometimes called Love Lane) were the first to play there in 1876, followed later by several other local cricket teams.

The 'Rovers' played on the area where the bowling greens are now situated. Cricket must have been played on both levels in view of the number of clubs wanting a ground. In the boardroom at Edgeley Park for many years was a framed balance sheet and fixture list for the first season 1883-84 . This valuable piece of history, along with any other club records, were all destroyed when the main stand was burned down in 1936. There were no matches featured in the local press for the opening season, due to the monopoly of Rugby - maybe they weren't yet organised to get a match report to the newspapers by the Tuesday deadline!

By now the Recreation Ground was being used by several football clubs i.e. Christ Church, which would have created problems with matches and maybe they wanted a 'clean' break from the Church team. A move

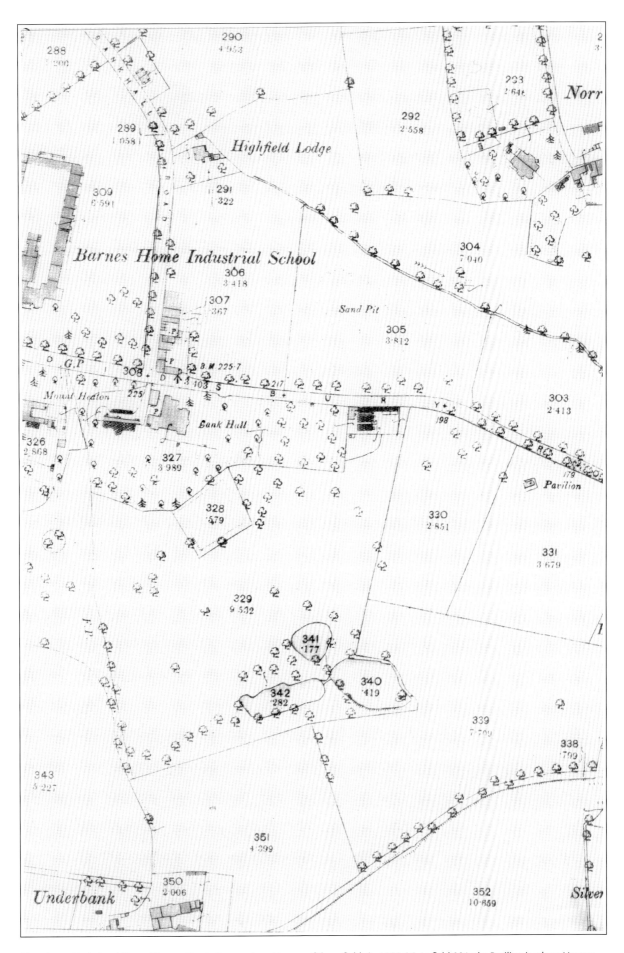

Map shows Underbank Farm, Heaton Norris Rovers played in one of these fields in 1885-86. In field 331, the Pavilion is where Heaton Mersey Cricket Club first started in 1879

was made for 1884-85 to Lomas's field, already used by Heaton Norris Wanderers Cricket Club. This was situated where the No. 1 Ring Spinning Mill was to be built in 1892 (now demolished) - just over the river Mersey from Brinksway. The area is now covered by a business park, and was referred to in the press simply as 'Brinksway'.

The 'Wanderers' had been in existence from the mid 1870s and had played on Heaton Norris Recreation Ground, but due to the congestion of teams based there, they had to find a new 'home' for the 1884 season. There was a cricket game in that summer of 1884, Heaton Norris Rovers v Heaton Norris Wanderers - no footballers in the Rovers side, so a bit of a mystery! It was not unusual for football to be played on cricket pitches i.e. 20 early Cup Finals at the Oval Ground.

In the 1884 summer, Messrs Whittle, Holden, Ashworth and Hewitt were still playing cricket for the Wycliffe team, although by now they had joined Heaton Norris Rovers F.C.

**The first report of an Association Football game in Stockport appeared in January 1884:**
'WYCLIFFE v BELMONT, ASSOCIATION - Wycliffe Congregational Church defeated Belmont on Saturday by three goals to one. Played on the Recreation Ground, Heaton Norris'

This season saw the first match reported in the press, played on October 11th, 1884. The short report in the *Cheshire County News* read:

**'Heaton Norris Rovers -v- Stalybridge (2nd team). Played on Saturday at Heaton Norris, and resulted in a victory for the visitors, who scored three goals to nil for Heaton Norris'**

Their next game the following Saturday v Christ Church (Heaton Norris), losing 1-0 on their opponents ground : 'A certain amount of ill-feeling was manifested, and the Christ Church captain decided to abandon the return match'. This situation was typical, as at best there may have been one umpire, usually selected by the home club, with no referee - disputes had to be settled between rival captains! A later 4-1 defeat at Stalybridge, saw the 'Rovers' arrive for the game without their goalkeeper and only 8 players!

The first time the Heaton Norris Rovers team was published was a game v Tame Valley (Dukinfield), played at home losing 2-0 : Whittle; Machin, Ashworth; Riley, Booth, Boardman; Holden, Simpson, Hewitt, Richardson, Clarke.

The first full match report of a game v one of several Church teams was in late November 1884:

**HEATON NORRIS ROVERS v OLD ST. GEORGE'S**
'These clubs met, for the first time this season, on Saturday, at Stalybridge. At ten minutes to four the Rovers put the ball in motion, and ten minutes after scored their first goal. Immediately after the kick off, they again lowered their opponents' colours, the forwards passing well, and carrying both goal-keeper and ball under the bar. The Dragons now pulled up, and with a combined rush carried the ball well into the visitors 25, where a well directed shot had the desired effect.
After half time, the Rovers had to play up-hill, but not withstanding this they resisted all the Dragons' attempts, and succeeded in adding two more goals to their score. One was disputed, it being doubtful whether the leather really went under owing to the darkness which was setting in soon after time was called, leaving the Rovers victors by three goals to one. Team - Forwards: Hewitt, Clarke, Simpson, Booth, and S. Riley; half-backs: Riley (captain), Whittle, and Gatler; full backs*: W. Hewitt, Machin, Stuart (goal)'

**\*sometimes still referred to as 'three quarter backs'**

It is most likely that the fixtures for the Rovers first season, 1883-84, would have been similar to this one - the report above implies the 2 clubs had met before. Apart from Christ Church, they had to travel (by train wherever possible) outside Stockport, to find opponents who played the Association game.

After one season at Heaton Norris Wanderers Cricket Ground, the club was on the move again for the 1885-86 season. Maybe the 'Wanderers' objected to the football season overlapping (still playing cricket in October) with their cricket or damage to the pitch, or the rent was too expensive! There must have been a problem, as the next ground was not well situated, at the end of a country lane! A few years later, the Wanderers formed their own football team, playing on the Recreation ground, not the cricket pitch!

The club's short trip to a new venue was the first time the 'Rovers' moved out of Heaton Norris to Heaton Mersey, to one of the 6 fields surrounding what was locally known as 'Chorlton's Farm', off Didsbury Road. Officially called Underbank Farm, with 84 acres run by Sarah Chorlton with her family of 2 sons and a daughter. The Chorlton family had been in the area from the 18th century and purchased the farm from Joseph Burgess.

**I have found where this farm was located** - Chorlton's Lane is now a combination of Branksome Road and Valley Road, the farm buildings next to what is now Mersey Vale Primary School. In the 1880s, the farm was not far from the Heaton Mersey East Junction of the railway line from Tiviot Dale Station. It is possible that the 'friendly' cricketers of Heaton Mersey Cricket Club (1879) let the players change in their nearby Pavilion - the other alternative would have been in one of the farms outbuildings!

Like many clubs, the Rovers started the new season with a game amongst themselves: 2 teams were chosen by Ed. Simpson (Capt.) and Ed. Whittle (Vice Capt.), the game kicked off at 3.30 with the former winning by 5-1.

For the first time there is evidence this season, that the club also had an 'A' side and occasionally brief match reports were featured i.e. Heaton Norris Rovers 2nd Team 1 v West Gorton Athletic (1st) 1.

One of the other clubs in the area simply called themselves Heaton Norris - in December 1885, the 2 teams met and the newspaper report read:

**'The return match between these clubs was played on Saturday on the Chorlton's Farm ground. Heaton Norris were assisted by four of the Christ Church club, whilst the Rovers were weakened by the absence of Ashworth, Talbot and Williamson. The home team were severely handicapped against their weighty opponents on the soft heavy ground, and the home backs had warm work in repelling the visitors rushes. Simpson however, changed positions with Whittle, and playing well up amongst his half-backs completely baffled the Norrisites throwing them 'off-side' time after time.**
**At half-time neither team had scored but shortly after the resumption, Whittle ran down and shot through. The game was fought very shibbornly, and just before time, when Riley senior had the goal at his mercy Heaton Norris claimed 'off-side'. There was no off-side about it, and of course it led to an abdication. The game however, proceeded, when the whistle blew the Rovers were again victorious by one goal to nil. Rovers team: Thomasson; Simpson (captain), Kelly; Hewitt, Richardson, Whitmore; Riley, Booth, Hewitt (J), Whittle and Clarke'**

**\* 'shot through' -Goal Nets were not introduced for another 5 years, initially only for major games - smaller teams couldn't afford the expense anyway!**

At the end of this season, these 2 clubs amalgamated. This fact is confirmed in 'The Football Encyclopaedia', written within living memory of the event. They were to play on the Heaton Norris ground next to the 'Ash Inn' (now 'Ash Hotel' re-built in 1901), Manchester Road, Heaton Chapel (Reuben Street ran alongside the cricket ground and still remains, but Kingsley Avenue, Horace Grove, Bournville Avenue and Selby Street now exist where the ground used to be). Agreement also had to be made with Heaton Norris Cricket Club - the *Cheshire County News* reporting that 'The Heaton Norris Cricket Club have kindly placed their ground on the Manchester Old Road at the disposal of the Rovers...'

The cricket club was founded c. 1860 and was a team of some prominence, as Heaton Norris appear in the

1875 fixture card of Stockport CC. In a match v Crewe Regalia in May 1885, the team including 2 members of the Heaton Norris Rovers football team - Kelly and Riley opened the batting for them. Therefore there was already a relationship with the organisation (full title - Heaton Norris Cricket & Association Football Club) on Manchester Road and most of the footballers would know each other anyway in the area. The Heaton Norris football team had only been in existence for one season.

In the 1880s, the country was nearer than today in Stockport, the air fresher - we would arrive at the ground by foot, or perhaps 'Hansom' cab if more affluent. Not worried by traffic, and the ground, when we reach it is open without stands - more like a meadow. There is plenty of room, you can wander round the touchline, or behind the goals. If there are more than a few hundred people watching, it must be a game of some importance.

When the players appear, it is difficult for us looking at old photographs, to take seriously the athletes of the period. Off the field, their dress suggests stuffiness and stiffness; on the field, they seem to us unconvincing fancy dress and they are not helped by the ornamental whiskers and the studio poses! We would probably feel differently, watching them in the flesh, as they prepare to start the game. They were vigorous physical specimens, brought up to believe in the moral value of bodily fitness and hard effort!

No doubt they moved easily and gracefully enough, in spite of the strange costume - which looked odd for football! They wear long trousers or knickerbockers, they have tight jerseys, perhaps striped, perhaps with a crest on the breast, and on their heads some players wear caps. The boots are ordinary strong walking boots, and according to laws, they must have no iron and no projecting nails!

For the 1886-87 season, the first mention of the clubs colours - referred to as 'the dark blues' and were sometimes called Heaton Norris on the Ash. The following 'piece' appeared in the press before the start of the new season:

**'HEATON NORRIS ROVERS TEAMS ON HEATON NORRIS CRICKET GROUND. A very attractive list of matches, including the Manchester Junior Cup Comptetion. The Rovers being considered the leading Association players in Stockport, they hope to receive the public patronage for what will surely prove interesting and exciting games during the winter months'**

| Date 1886 | | | Ground | F.A. |
|---|---|---|---|---|
| October | 2nd | Crewe Villa | Home ... | 4-2 |
| " | " 9th | New Mills | Away | |
| " | " 16th | Strines (Marple) | Home | |
| " | " 23rd | Denton Rovers | Away ... | 3-0 |
| " | " 30th | Bradford (Manchester) | Home ... | 12-1 |
| November | 6th | Bollington Cross Rovers | Away ... | 1-1 |
| " | " 13th | West Gorton Athletic | Home | |
| " | " 20th | Denton Rovers | Home ... | 2-1 |
| " | " 27th | Manchester Senior Cup | Home | |
| December | 4th | Bollington Cross Rovers | Home ... | 2-1 |
| " | " 11th | New Mills | Home | 1-1 |
| " | " 18th | Hayfield | Away | |
| " | " 25th | Ryecroft (Manchester) | Home | |
| **1887** | | | | |
| January | 1st | Strines (Marple) | Away | 2-4 |
| " | " 8th | West Gorton Athletic | Away | |
| " | " 15th | Macclesfield Sunday School | Home | 1-1 |
| " | " 22nd | New Zealand Wanderers (A) | Away | 10-2 |
| " | " 29th | Gorton Villa (A) | Home | |
| February | 5th | Manchester South End | Home | |
| " | " 12th | Gorton (A) | Away | |
| " | " 19th | Bradford (Manchester) | Away | |
| " | " 26th | Macclesfield Sunday School | Away | |
| March | 5th | Hayfield | Home | |
| " | " 12th | Gorton Villa (A) | Away | |
| " | " 19th | Manchester South End | Away | |
| " | " 21st | Ryecroft (Manchester) | Away | |

Heaton Norris Rovers played their first ever competitive match in November v Kearsley Olympic (Bolton) in the Manchester & District Cup at home.

For season 1887-88, there were several developments for the club. The Rovers started the season at a **previously undiscovered 'extra' ground -** the *Cheshire Daily Echo* in early September: 'Heaton Norris Rovers have left the Ash Inn ground and moved to a field in Manchester Road'. After a few weeks, another new playing venue, complete with a slope, to locally named 'Wilkes' Field', off Belmont Street, Wellington Road North, officially known as Carr's Field, owned by William Wilkes - where Lloyd Street and All Saints Primary School now stand. The press always referred to the pitch as the 'Wellington Road North' ground.

There must have been a serious problem to leaving the 'Ash Inn', as the club had to find this 'temporary' base on Manchester Road. Players would now be wanting some payment for playing, as professionalism had been approved in 1885, for 'lost' working hours on a Saturday. The club would now require an enclosed ground at 'Wilkes' Field', so that a small admission charge could be made - no doubt the fencing would have been completed by the players. Therefore attendances could now be recorded, the largest being 2,000 in a match v Oldham, as well as crowds of 1,300 and 1,000.

Amongst the playing ranks of the Rovers were now amazingly 4 sets of brothers: Messrs Broadbent, Simpson, Riley and Kelly.

The first game v Crewe Excelsior on the new pitch came about in comic circumstances. This fixture was not 'on the card', although Heaton Norris's secretary had written to Crewe earlier in the week, inviting them for a match. No reply received, so it was assumed no game - Crewe arrived to find no opposition! The Heaton team 'rounded up' some players and kicked off at 3.30pm - providing the few spectators with an entertaining 8-6 win!

The newspaper report of the game at Rainow 'paints' a typical picture of the nature of matches in the 1880s:

**'The Heaton Norris team travelled in a wagonette on Saturday to play on the Rainow Ground. They made the journey to Bollington in good time, but here on account of the steep road they had to alight and tramp it to Rainow, arriving at 3.45 in not the best of condition. The game was all in favour of the home team who, playing with the wind scored three goals in the first-half. The second-half was played in darkness and Rainow rushed two more through, thus winning 5 goals to nil. Rainow entertained their opponents to tea in the schoolroom after the match. The teams meet again on Saturday on the Rover's ground'**

**FOOTNOTE:** Having arrived at Bollington, the players then had to climb up Windmill Lane and Lidgetts Lane, walk through Rainow village and up the main road to a bleak field on the corner of Smith Lane, nearest to Rainow. The home team consisted of mill-workers from a large mill in the small village!

Not surprisingly, with the team in 'better condition', they easily defeated the 'team from the hills' by 5-2!

Season 1888-89 (Football League founded), it appears the club dropped 'Rovers' off their title, and

Schoolroom in Rainow, where Heaton Norris Rovers were entertained after the match in season 1887-88

like the team of old just called themselves Heaton Norris - probably thinking they were now the premier club in the district! For the past few years there had been a reserve X1, but now an 'A' team also operated - even some of these games were reported in the press.

This season saw Heaton Norris move to the 7th ground in their short history, Green Lane - at last the club had found somewhere that would be their 'home' for the next 14 years. The club played behind the 'Nursery Inn' - first recorded as a 'beer house' in 1869 and took its name from the market garden district of the area. The teams colours were now red and white stripes.

There was already a bowling green directly behind the pub, the football playing area beyond (now houses on Nursery Road) was just an open field when Heaton Norris first arrived. The pitch was soon fenced off, as an entrance fee was a priority - turnstiles would have followed. After one season, a wooden stand was erected on the Heaton Mersey side of the site by the players - the Stockport end a raised bank was installed - later at the Heaton Moor end, a large uncovered terrace and smaller terrace nearest to the bowling green. The players changed upstairs in a barn (now demolished), alongside the pub and walked round the bowling green to the pitch - the ground was very full with 6,000 inside!

When I wrote 'The History of Stockport County A.F.C.' in 1966, I visited the 'Nursery Inn' on the 'off chance' there may have been an old photograph still there. A week later, the landlord rang to tell me an old framed team picture had been found in the bowling hut behind the pub - no date or names on it! I found an old supporter, Mr. Clark, who lived in a little terraced house, dropping down off Stockport market, who recognised 4 of the players, confirming the date.

This veteran fan, had happy memories of the 'Green Lane days'. 'When I was a boy of 9 or 10, I used to wait outside the ground with about 10 other boys, while waiting for our fathers to come out of the 'Nursery' after having 1 or 2 pints, and after bargaining with the man on the turnstiles, we all ducked under for a shilling!'(5p)

The first game at the new Green Lane ground appears to be a 3-1 defeat to Marple, before a crowd of 1000. The press judged the match to be Heaton Norris v the Marple "Umpire", due to his bias decisions!

It is interesting to note that when the club played Denton 'A' at home, the Denton team were referred to as the 'Hatters', some years before County - the hatting industry had spread to neighbouring towns by now.

The club's record for the season 1889-90 was: Played 34, Won 18, Drawn 4, Lost 12 - scoring 88 goals with 48 against. The expenses for the season being £166 2s 3d, whilst the income had been £171 12s 7d.

On 24th May 1890, the *Cheshire Daily Echo* announced: 'The Stockport County AFC - a rather ambitious title, certainly - is to be the new designation of the Heaton Norris Club'. The new name, was as a result of Stockport becoming a County Borough in April 1889, and showed the teams ambitions for the future.

County were not on their own in wanting to take the town's name. Also starting in 1890-91 season were Stockport Association.

'Nursery Inn', Green Lane, County's ground behind the Inn from 1888-1902. The barn can be seen where the players changed

Stockport County's first game under the town name was a 5-3 defeat away at Hurst (near Ashton), on 6th September, 1890.

Even though the club had been in existence for 7 years, there were still problems with certain matches: County travelled to New Mills with only 8 players, including 3 second team members, 3 substitutes were obtained from the home side. 'Mistake in carriage the costumes of the Norrisites were over carried and the

team had to play in their ordinary attire'. Not surprisingly, County lost the game 4-1!

For this season, the first 'Gentleman' player appeared in County's team - Doctor Thomas Parkyn Blades, aged 24, who played at centre-half or occasionally a centre-forward and Captain. Dr. Blades came from Kirby Stephen, Westmorland. He qualified as a doctor at Edinburgh University and became a home surgeon in Stockport Infirmary. He was a good sportsman -

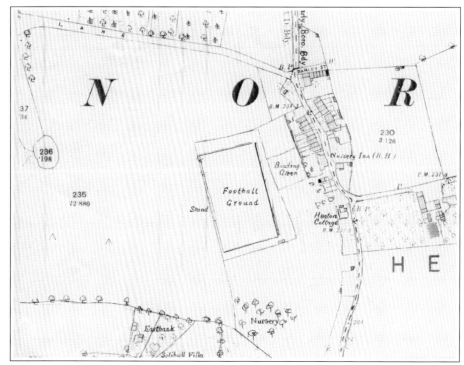

Map of the Green Lane ground in the 1890s

The First Picture of Stockport County

Pictured in their red & white stripes behind the 'Nursery Inn' just 7 years after the club was formed. Believed to have been taken before their first home game in September 1890. The clubs first 'gentleman' player Dr. Blades in the white shirt

being an excellent footballer, golfer, boxer, all round athlete and horseman.

Dr. Blades played regularly for the club for 2 full seasons, his last outing being the 3rd game of season 1892-93. Pressure of work forced him to leave the club - a big loss to County! He had started a practice in Romiley and moved to the village in 1892. He was a very clever man, a doctor, a surgeon of skill and healer of the sick - highly respected in Romiley and often completed his 'rounds' by horse.

He was to join Romiley Golf Club, and was elected Captain in 1902-03 and again in 1909-11 - followed later by becoming Chairman of the Board of Directors from 1916 to his death in 1918 aged 52 from

pneumonia, during the flu epidemic at the end of the war. Dr. Blades was sadly missed by the community as a doctor and an outstanding member of Romiley Golf Club - to this day, 2 competitions are still played for in his name!

County played a 'rare' competitive match in the 2nd Round of the Manchester Senior Cup v Heaton Park, January 1891. The Manchester club had choice of ground and went for Green Lane, arriving with a weakened team and complained to the referee about the state of the pitch after heavy rain. This was acknowledged and Heaton Park's protest was likely to be upheld, the game still went ahead! County won the match 14-0, as expected the objection was upheld and a 'replay' arranged. Heaton Park brought only 6

County's first 'gentleman' player Dr. Blades

players and 'scratched' and agreed to play an 'exhibition' match after persuading 5 spectators to join them!

With a 3-2 win v Royton in Round 3 (record 2500 crowd), saw County play Newton Heath (later Manchester United who joined League Division 1 in 1892) in the Semi-Final. The game was played at Hyde Road, Ardwick (Manchester City's ground before Maine Road) before a crowd of 5,000, losing 3-1. The County side: Urmston; Gaskell, Ferguson; Pixton, Dr. Blades, Jepson; Simpson, Roberts, Smith, Upton, Wright.

After 8 seasons of mainly 'friendly' matches, County were elected into the Football Combination, in its second year, for 1891-92. The club soon found it a struggle in this competition, losing their opening fixture 3-0 v Macclesfield at home, followed by 5 more defeats! The Green Lane crowds increased, and ranged between 2,000 and 4,000. The first season in League football finished as follows:

### THE COMBINATION

| | P | W | D | L | Goals | Pts |
|---|---|---|---|---|---|---|
| Everton Reserve | 22 | 17 | 2 | 3 | 99-20 | 36 |
| Northwich Victoria | 22 | 15 | 1 | 6 | 84-25 | 31 |
| Macclesfield | 22 | 15 | 0 | 7 | 52-38 | 30 |
| Stoke Swifts | 22 | 13 | 1 | 8 | 49-29 | 27 |
| Buxton | 22 | 11 | 3 | 8 | 35-30 | 25 |
| Wrexham | 22 | 9 | 2 | 11 | 45-65 | 20 |
| Chirk | 22 | 7 | 5 | 10 | 48-56 | 19 |
| Gorton Villa | 22 | 8 | 3 | 11 | 41-51 | 19 |
| Chester | 22 | 8 | 3 | 11 | 52-61 | 19 |
| Leek | 22 | 8 | 0 | 14 | 46-62 | 16 |
| Stockport County | 22 | 7 | 2 | 13 | 29-44 | 16 |
| Denton | 22 | 2 | 2 | 18 | 25-124 | 6 |

The worst defeat for County next season was an 8-1 thrashing, away to Bury (joined League Division 11 in 1894) in an F.A. Cup Qualifying match. A big improvement in the League, however, finishing in 6th place.

Season 1893-94 saw Stockport County trying again in the F.A. Cup Qualifying Competition: Round 1 - Bootle walk-over; Round 2 - County 2 Tranmere Rovers 1; Round 3 - County 3 Wrexham 2, Replayed as the Welsh side complained about the pitch, County 7 Wrexham 0; Round 4 - County 0 Crewe Alexandra 0, Replay Crewe 1 County 2.

So County were through to the First Round Proper, with a home tie v Burton Wanderers (elected to League Division 11 next season). Green Lane's largest crowd to date of 4,500, saw Stockport lose by 1-0.

In June 1894, the club held its AGM in the Conservative Club, Short Street, Heaton Norris and discussed the big drop in gates for the season. There was not a single game outside of the Combination fixtures which had paid - only 4 within the league had met the club's expenses! The previous season £185 was paid in wages, whereas this season's wages amounted to £345. With league games and 'friendlies', Stockport had played 41 matches, won 18, drawn 11 and lost only 12.

The Lancashire League had extended its membership to 14 clubs and there was still one more vacancy - 6 other teams applied but County received 7 votes from the 10 clubs represented at the meeting. To be ready for the demands of higher quality football, the club introduced 15 players, who had not played the previous season! First campaign in the new league was as follows:

### LANCASHIRE LEAGUE

| | P | W | D | L | Goals | Pts |
|---|---|---|---|---|---|---|
| Fairfield | 26 | 17 | 3 | 6 | 68-32 | 37 |
| Blackpool | 26 | 16 | 2 | 8 | 89-34 | 34 |
| Nelson | 26 | 14 | 5 | 7 | 75-45 | 33 |
| Southport Central | 26 | 13 | 4 | 8 | 68-42 | 32 |
| Fleetwood Rangers | 26 | 13 | 6 | 7 | 62-49 | 32 |
| Bacup | 26 | 13 | 5 | 8 | 65-55 | 31 |
| Chorley | 26 | 11 | 3 | 12 | 69-56 | 25 |
| West Manchester | 26 | 10 | 5 | 11 | 61-63 | 25 |
| Stockport County | 26 | 10 | 5 | 11 | 53-69 | 25 |
| South Shore | 26 | 9 | 6 | 11 | 59-45 | 24 |
| Rossendale | 26 | 10 | 3 | 13 | 51-51 | 23 |
| Accrington | 26 | 10 | 2 | 14 | 62-63 | 22 |
| Clitheroe | 26 | 7 | 1 | 18 | 61-93 | 15 |
| Heywood Central | 26 | 3 | 0 | 23 | 28-171 | 6 |

Prior to the start of 1896-97 season, County's new signings included the excellent goalkeeper Joe Lee and outside-left Arthur Lee, both from Earlestown, plus half-back Thomas Hall from Macclesfield. Tommy Hall was known as 'Bute' Hall, due to his good looks. He started his football career with Macclesfield St.Georges' Club for one season, before playing for Macclesfield in the Combination for 2 years, Mr. George Ellis having 'booked' him at the 'Gransmore Hotel', Fairfield. In 1900, Tommy was transferred to local rivals Glossop North End - having stayed for 2 years, he was back in County's ranks for the start of 1903-04 season. For the first 5 years playing for Stockport, he only failed with 4 penalty conversions. Following 11 years service, he was awarded a testimonial match in 1907.

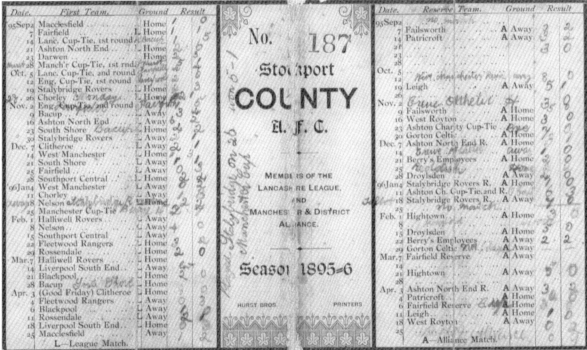

Season 1897-98, saw many changes to the Lancashire League: Fleetwood Rangers, Rossendale and West Manchester dropping out - 5 new teams were admitted: Horwich, Middleton, Rochdale and Wigan County and the well-known but short-lived New Brighton Tower, financed by the New Brighton Tower & Recreation Co. strictly as a commercial enterprise - with the sole intention of being a top Football League team!

The signings by County of Worrall from Nelson and Joe Foster from Coppenhall (Crewe) were important additions to the club. Other new players were Parkins (Mexborough) and Roger Bridges brother from Chorley.

Manchester City made their only visit to Green Lane this season - 'Second League v Lancashire League created a lot of interest'. County lead 1-0 at half-time, winning the 'friendly' emphatically by 4-1!

There was great success in Cup competitions this season. County had reached the last qualifying round of the F.A. Cup, before losing 1-0 at Green Lane to New Brighton Tower.

Turning to the Manchester Senior Cup in February, Bolton Wanderers (League Division 1) were defeated by 2-1. A Tommy Hall penalty was enough to beat Glossop North End (elected into the League Division 11 at the end of this season) after a replay. Stockport County were now through to the Senior Cup Final v Manchester City - between these 2 games, Arthur Lea was transferred to Bolton who 'lent' him back to County for the Final!

Stockport County Reserves 1895-96

Winners of the Manchester & District Amateur Cup. This picture was taken in the field next to the Green Lane ground, in the background is the back of the wooden stand

The Final was played at the home of the Manchester Athletic Club at Fallowfield - 5 years earlier an F. A. Cup Final was played there amongst chaotic scenes, when 45,000 forced their way into the enclosure: Wolves beat Everton 1-0. The cost of the journey for fans by wagonette was 1s. 3d. or by rail at 6d. return fare from Tiviot Dale to Fallowfield Station. By far the largest crowd County had played in front of (15,000) saw City win 4-0 but Stockport lodged an appeal, arguing that City's outside-left Dougal was ineligible. The Manchester F.A. ruled that the player was not officially registered to play and over-ruled City's appeal that County's Arthur Lea was not qualified to play!

Having lost so heavily and the travelling costs, again resulted in a lot smaller crowd of 4,000 for the replay held at Bank Street, Clayton - Newton Heath's (later Manchester United) Ground. Two goals by Joe Foster gave County an amazing 2-1 win and their first major trophy! In City's ranks was the famous Welshman Billy Meredith, who also went on to be a brilliant player for Manchester United.

The 2 teams lined up as follows in the victorious match:

**MANCHESTER CITY**

Chappell

Moffatt          Read

Munn          Smith          Holmes

Meredith     S. Smith     Gillespie     Whitehead     Leonard

-0-

A. Lee     Foster     Worrall     Heyes     Bridge

Bolton          Hall          Mann

Wainwright          Blears

Kitchen

**STOCKPORT COUNTY**

## Stockport County v Manchester City

Manchester Senior Cup Final at Fallowfield, 1898, a section of how the crowd would have looked at the game.
The F.A. Cup Final was played at this athletics stadium in 1893, with 'recorded' 45,000 gate, when Wolves beat Everton 1-0

# Winners of the Manchester Senior Cup

Pictured in front of the 'Railway' Hotel' are: Back row H. Blears, J. Wainwright, G. Kitchen, T. Hall, R. Mann, W. Bolton, Fred Stewart (Manager). Front row R. Bridge, H. Heyes, A. Worrall (Captain), J. Foster, A. Lee

For season 1898-99, County's performances in the Lancashire League were modest - finishing in 6th place. Signings during the season included Betteley and Chesworth from Nantwich, and Moores from Rock Ferry (Merseyside).

There was, however, further success to follow back in the Manchester Senior Cup. County's progress was again subject to controversy - this time in the semi, rather than the final. In March 1899, Stockport met old rivals Ashton North End at neutral Fallowfield. County won 2-1, but Ashton protested, both about the ground and about 'something wrong with the goalposts and crossbars' - basically any excuse to try and gain a replay! Their protest was upheld, but justice was done and a 2-0 victory for County resulted.

In the Final, County were up against First Division Bury at Ardwick (Manchester City's ground before Maine Road). A crowd of 6,000 saw the 'hatters' come from 2-0 down in the last 15 minutes to score through Artie Goddard and Frank Chesworth to earn a replay. Again the replay was staged at Clayton - County retained the Cup 2-1, with goals from Chesworth and Billy Betteley.

Maybe in view of the club's success in winning the Manchester Senior Cup again, County applied to join League Division 11 - the voting went as follows: Lougborough 28, Chesterfield 27 and Middlesbrough 17, elected. Blackpool 15, Stockport County 11, Chorley 7, Wigan County 7, Coventry City 0 and Ashton North End 0, not elected.

New recruits for 1899-1900 campaign were Andrew Limond from Wigan County and Percy Pickford from Macclesfield, plus keeping the majority of the existing players. New entries into the Lancashire League were Blackpool, Darwen, White Star Wanderers, Earlestown and South Liverpool - Ashton North End and Halliwell withdrew. The admission charges to the Green Lane ground were 4d and 6d, according to whether you went under the covered stand or terraced areas.

In order for the Second Team to have a full fixture list, they took part both in the Central Lancashire and the Stockport and District Leagues. The strength of the Stockport competition can be seen by the clubs taking part: Hyde, Macclesfield, Buxton Reserve, Whaley Bridge, Fairfield, Poynton, Disley and Bollington.

Another unusual match during this season took place in the January v Haydock. The game was played in torrential rain and after 65 minutes with County 5-1 in front, Haydock wanted the referee to abandon the match - when the ref. refused, 6 Haydock players

Lancashire League Champions 1899-1900

Photographed on the 'Nursery Inn' bowling green. Back row Hall, Johnson, Moores. Middle row Goddard, Foster, Wainwright, Patterson, Chesworth, Betteley. Front row Harvey, Axon

walked off! Play continued for another 15 minutes, Stockport scoring another 4 goals, before the ref. finally abandoned it! The Lancashire League ordered that Haydock should return to Green Lane and play the final 10 minutes - not surprisingly they didn't bother!

Having won 21 of their 28 matches, County were crowned Champions of the Lancashire League - the Cup was displayed in the window of 'Froggatt's Funeral Establishment' on Heaton Lane and later at the 'Nursery Inn' - maybe now, Stockport were ready for a higher class of football. As Champions, the club played a Rest of the League X1 at Green Lane in April, winning 4-1. County's team: Moores; Johnston, Wainwright; Hall, Limond, Pickford; Foster, Parker, Patterson, Chesworth, Betteley. The League was represented by: Lee (Haydock); Bunce (Rochdale), Ostick (Chorley); Brown (Blackpool), Liversey (Darwen), Johnson (Stalybridge Rovers); Johnson (Rochdale), Baxendale (Southport Central), Lawson (Stalybridge Rovers), Hulligan (Liverpool White Star), Tinsley (Horwich).

The receipts for Stockport County's home matches amounted to £999 17s 9d, but expenses were £1195 9s 11d, leaving a shortfall of £196 12s 2nd.

A special evening was arranged for 23rd April 1900, at the Armoury, for the presentation of the Lancashire Cup and medals to the players. The Mayor (Councillor T. Webb) received the cup and the Captain of the team James Wainwright replied, expressing the thanks of the players. The entertainment included a full band, whose services had been secured by permission of Colonel Carrington. Songs were rendered by Mr. Joseph Knott and Mr. A. Boyd (humorist), 2 admirable concertina solos by Mr. Horbury, Corporal Harry King contributed a clarinet solo before the dancing got underway!

The AGM of 1900 was held at the Mechanics' Institution - the main subject on the agenda was whether to apply again for Second Division membership. A resolution was also discussed to the effect that Stockport Rugby Club should be approached for the amalgamation of 2 of the oldest Rugby and Association teams in the town to play at Edgeley Park. County's application to join the League was successful: Barnsley 29 votes, Stockport County 28, Blackpool 24, elected. Doncaster 5, Lougborough 3, Kettering 2, Stalybridge Rovers 1.

The Manager of the club was Fred Stewart, who had been involved with the administrative side at County for 7 years - he went on to become a successful Manager at Cardiff City in 1911.

Stockport County were now to play in the Football League for the first time. Famous clubs in Division 11 then were: Newton Heath (Manchester United), Woolwich Arsenal, Burnley and Small Heath (Birmingham City) - there was however, a long hard struggle ahead over the coming seasons!

The well-known amateur player, Martin John Earp, was signed for £100 from Sheffield Wednesday. He captained the victorious Yorkshire side in the F.A. Cup Final v Wolverhampton Wanderers in 1896, and was an all-round sportsman and athlete, who also played tennis and other games. The right-back, an International, joined County at the age of 28 and was remembered by the fact that Mr. Earp ('gentleman' player) objected to changing with the rest of the team at the 'Nursery' but instead 'stripped' in the 'George Hotel', Wellington Road North - travelling to the Green Lane Ground by 'Hansom Cab' (a 2 wheeled cab in which the driver's seat is behind the body, the reins passing over the hooded top). However, in January 1901, Mr. Earp had left the club. He went to South Africa, to join Major General Baden-Powell's Police - 'He did not inform the committee of his intention to leave the team'!

Stockport County's first ever League match was away to Leicester Fosse (Leicester City) on 1st September 1900. The team left by train from Tiviot Dale Station at 9.45 and were joined by their new Captain John Earp at Nottingham - arriving at Leicester about 1p.m. Around 7,000 watched the game which ended a 2-2 draw. The County team that day: Moores; Earp, Wainwright; Pickford, Limond, Harvey; Betteley, Foster, Patterson, Smith, Stansfield. The first victory came on the following Monday, a 1-0 win at Burslem Port Vale. Due to injuries, the club signed Preston North End player Stansfield for the princely sum of £12 10s!

The club's first season in the Football League ended thus:

### FOOTBALL LEAGUE - DIVISION 11

| | | P | W | D | L | Goals | Pts |
|---|---|---|---|---|---|---|---|
| 1 | Grimsby Town | 34 | 20 | 9 | 5 | 60-33 | 49 |
| 2 | Small Heath | 34 | 19 | 10 | 5 | 57-24 | 48 |
| 3 | Burnley | 34 | 20 | 4 | 10 | 53-29 | 44 |
| 4 | New Brighton Tower | 34 | 17 | 8 | 9 | 57-38 | 42 |
| 5 | Glossop North End | 34 | 15 | 8 | 11 | 51-33 | 38 |
| 6 | Middlesbrough | 34 | 15 | 7 | 12 | 50-40 | 37 |
| 7 | Woolwich Arsenal | 34 | 15 | 6 | 13 | 39-35 | 36 |
| 8 | Lincoln City | 34 | 13 | 7 | 14 | 43-39 | 33 |
| 9 | Burslem Port Vale | 34 | 11 | 11 | 12 | 45-47 | 33 |
| 10 | Newton Heath | 34 | 14 | 4 | 16 | 42-38 | 32 |
| 11 | Leicester Fosse | 34 | 11 | 10 | 13 | 39-37 | 32 |
| 12 | Blackpool | 34 | 12 | 7 | 15 | 33-58 | 31 |
| 13 | Gainsborough Trinity | 34 | 10 | 10 | 14 | 45-60 | 30 |
| 14 | Chesterfield Town | 34 | 9 | 10 | 15 | 46-58 | 28 |
| 15 | Barnsley | 34 | 11 | 5 | 18 | 47-60 | 27 |
| 16 | Walsall | 34 | 7 | 13 | 14 | 40-56 | 27 |
| 17 | Stockport County | 34 | 11 | 3 | 20 | 38-68 | 25 |
| 18 | Burton United | 34 | 8 | 4 | 22 | 34-66 | 20 |

*Grimsby Town and Small Heath promoted to Division 1. New Brighton Tower Resigned. Walsall failed to gain re-election, their places taken by Bristol City and Doncaster Rovers.*

The idea of moving to Edgeley Park to join Stockport Rugby Club had been discussed at the AGM back in 1900 - in November that year, County officials met with Wilsons Brewery, who had just bought the land with a view to leasing the ground. Eventually, County

County (Champions) v Rest of Lancashire League

Pictured in April 1900. Back row Johnston, Hall, Moores, Limond, Harvey. Middle row Pickford, Foster, Patterson, Wainwright, Parker, Betteley. Front row Goddard, Chesworth. Only known photo inside the Green Lane ground - top left is the wooden stand & in the background is the large raised bank

Martin John Earp, County's first International player

left Green Lane in 1902 - the old ground was used by the Reserve team before later being sold for housing.

At the end of season 1903-04, County failed to gain re-election, but having won the Lancashire Combination, were back into League Division 11, due to the First and Second Divisions being enlarged from 18 to 20 clubs. From season 1905-06 onwards, Stockport County have remained members of the Football League - with a few ups and downs along the way!

Early football teams to appear in the press were: Marple 1 v Stretford 2 (1 disputed goal), Christ Church 1 v Hurdsfield (Macclesfield) 1, Newhall Rangers 5 v Macclesfield Sunday School 5.

Plans were drawn up in **1884** for **Stockport Swimming Baths** on St. Petersgate. There was to be a 1$^{st}$ class plunge bath 90' x 30' with a gallery. Separate Ladies plunge bath 40' x 18'. 42 private baths and Turkish baths on the first floor. The building was a free classic design with terra cotta used for architectural dressings. The total cost was £5000 and due for completion in the summer of 1885.

Stockport's Water Polo team photographed in 1904

The following article by a new reporter appeared at the start of the 1885-86 football season:

### FOOTBALL NOTES
'It is evident that this old English pastime is once more coming to the front. It will be remembered by the lovers of the game that Stockport, some years past could boast of strong organisations in the borough and its vicinity; but an unfortunate accident happened by which a young man, one of the players in the Stockport team, lost his life, the effect of this mishap being the extinction of these clubs.
However, the love for testing supremacy in the field still exists amongst the younger members of the

masculine community of the town, if the establishing of new clubs is anything to go by, and judging from the number and the quarters whereat they are being formed, it may safely be said that in the matter of football Stockport augurs well to eclipse any attempt previously in this direction.

First in the field we find Heaton Norris, with an association club in connection with their cricket club and we fully expect it will become a strong one, inasmuch as it possesses likely members to attain that end, 'coaching' being the only requirement. This step on the part of Heaton Norris seems to have prompted the Stockport club to follow suit, a meeting having been called for the purpose of promoting a similar object. Undoubtedly the general public will appreciate football as played under the association code and rules, and these two premier clubs have done well to have chosen this mode of playing.

Let us hope the community at large will show their appreciation. There have been also one or two clubs organised which play 'Rugby' but sooner or later, this game will finally give way to the modernised and less brutal enjoyment now being countenanced by the Heaton Norris and Stockport clubs.

Heaton Norris, although defeated, have cause to be satisfied with regard to the strides made by their team. The 'fight' they showed against Whaley Bridge on Saturday was everything that could be desired under the circumstances. They had 'hard lines' on many occasions, the ball skimming the goal-posts of their opponents, finishing up with 'shooting a goal just after the whistle had gone. However, they have been taught a lesson or two by this encounter. As an instance of this we may say that when arguing about a foul, the home team stole a march upon them by landing a goal whilst the Heaton Norris men were thus engaged, the whistle not having been sounded. Better luck next time.

Heaton Norris Rovers were also vanquished by that strong club, Manchester Clifford; but the result corroborates my opinion that this youthful club (although one of the oldest in Stockport as an association) is fairly strong, the result being four goals to three'.
DRIBBLER

FOOTNOTE: The association team did not happen until 1890-91. Heaton Norris only lasted one season (see Stockport County section) - re the match v Whaley Bridge, several members of the Heaton Norris team had never played football before - hardly surprising they lost 6-0!

Up to the late 18th century, Poynton was a small agricultural community - its farmers, small holders, craftsmen and labourers renting their property from their squires, various members of the Warren family, who resided at Poynton Hall, near to the present Poynton Pool. Sir George Warren, who died in 1801, not only greatly enlarged his park, created the Pool and rebuilt the Hall, but began, through his agents, to exploit the coal which had been raised since the 16th

## Poynton Cricket Club in 1904

Back row J. Walters, A. Wilson, J. Wild, J.R. Potts, L. Potts, A. Griffiths, J. Needham, E. Wood. Front row E. Singleton, E.M. Frosch, A. Clayton, A. Farguarson, G. Poole, H. Potts seated on 18th century St. George's Chapel benches

century in Poynton, and in the separate manor of Worth - owned by the Downes family. In 1791, George Warren purchased the manor of Worth.

In the 19th century, and indeed up to 1935, coalmining became the dominant activity in a population which increased from 620 persons in 1801 to 3,944 in 1931. The Warren Bulkeley's for a short time, and then the Vernon family, from 1826, acquired the Poynton estate through marriage - their main residence being at Sudbury, near Uttoxeter - they only resided in Poynton for short periods of time. The Hall was allowed to be demolished, but a large, modern mansion was built at the Towers for them to use.

The recognised date for the start of **Poynton Cricket Club** (now Poynton Sports Club) is **1885**, although there had already been a lot of cricket history in the village. Lord Vernon provided the intitial encouragement for the sport around 1850 - his Lordship gave his hall servants and local villagers land near his Towers home on which to play cricket together.

 The first recorded instance of an organised match was in 1868, when Poynton Vernon (the club's first name) (116) played a game v Heaton Mersey Sunday School (46). In June, 1872, Poynton visited Sudbury and lost by 22 runs to 53. In the early days, they either played on a rota basis, or alternated due to underground coal shift work. For example, in 1873, 31 different men played in 3 consecutive games! In the 1960s, when I was a playing member of Poynton CC, there was a one-off revival of these historic matches, when we sent a team to Sudbury.

The present cricket ground was made available by Lord Vernon in 1873, and the first known captain was E.T. Everett. In May, 1879, the 'Stockport Advertiser' published in full the first official score-card, when Poynton who scored 108, defeated Marple, on 57, by 51 runs - half of the Poynton team consisted of miners. The club had 9 more fixtures that season, 6 of them were at home: Heaton Norris Victoria, (Pott) Shrigley Vale, Heaton Norris Wanderers, Sudbury, Royal Oak and Hazel Grove. In the last v the 'Grove', Poynton scored only 8, including 7 'ducks'.

In 1880, a 2nd X1 was formed, but better fixtures were not forthcoming until the facilities were improved by the erection of a pavilion in 1880 - after their appeal for funds had been published in St. George's Church magazine......'The building will be an ornament to the village, and a great encouragement to those who are striving to provide innocent amusement for the villagers in their leisure hours'. This raised £80 and the building was completed the same year.

In 1892, Lord Vernon gave land adjoining the club for use as a football field. The following year, club subscriptions increased from 2/6d. to 3/6d.

**Poynton Amateurs Football Club** were formed in **1892**. Although there is no record of where they played in the formative years, a membership card for the 1912-13 season reveals that their ground was Poynton CC. Amongst the clubs the football team played were: India Mills, Lindow, Great Moor, Vernon Amateurs, Waterloo, Christy's Heaviley Sunday School and Handforth United.

In the middle 1890s, the irrepressible Lancashire and England all-rounder, Johnny Briggs played several times for Poynton - Prestbury and Macclesfield were dismissed for 12 and 15 respectively. The fixtures also included: Northenden, Whaley Bridge, Stockport Congregational, West Levenshulme, Cheadle Hulme, Macclesfield Parkside and Hazel Grove.

It was in 1897, that the landlord of the 'Butley Ash' laughed at Poynton cricketers dropping in for 'refreshments' on their way to play the mighty Macclesfield. Scornfully, he offered a gallon of beer per man if they won - the smile was wiped off his face when the lads returned, having dismissed Macclesfield for just 9 runs!

In May 1907 the Bowling Green was laid and opened by Captain Anson - a friend of Lord Vernon. In this same year, the club decided to try its hand at Lacrosse and give a demonstration on the cricket field. The finals of the Cheshire Lacrosse Association were played on the London Road Ground in June 1909. Whilst the lacrosse didn't survive, more successful was the introduction of tennis in 1912, when 2 grass courts were laid near to the present entrance to the ground.

In this Edwardian era, various social events were arranged, usually by the club Chairman, who 'doubled' as the Colliery Manager!

Leading players up to the start of the First World War were: E. Singleton, B.Birch, G.Poole, W. Dakin, V. Griffiths, Jimmy Needham and the Potts brothers. From arranging their own friendly matches, the club went into a Hazel Grove and District League.

During the War, club activities virtually ceased, although the bowling green continued to be maintained with the occasional match being played. One or two cricket games were arranged, including one in 1916 for the benefit of wounded soldiers who were at nearby Barlow Fold - converted to a war hospital.

The combination of the Billiards and Whist was proving to be a popular combination by the 1880s. A match with 8 players in each team - BILLIARDS: Edgeley 758, Mossley 618. WHIST: Edgeley 53, Mossley 84. 'During the evening both teams sat down to a good substantial tea, provided by the caretaker in a most satisfactory manner. A most enjoyable time was subsequently spent'

Cheshire cricket team had the rare chance to play Lancashire at Old Trafford this year - not surprisingly Lancashire (284) proved to be too strong for Cheshire (35 & 108). Briggs for Lancashire had the remarkable figures in the 1st innings of 16 overs, 7 for 10!

**Cheadle Golf Club** was established in 1885, making it the second oldest golf club in Cheshire - the oldest being the Royal Liverpool at Hoylake. The formation of the club was inspired by the deeds of golfing greats such as John Bell, James Braid and J.H. Taylor in the years 1883-84. Six of the local dignitaries, the Rev. F.A. Macdona (Rector of Cheadle), Messrs J.D., J.H. and C.D. Milne, Dr. W. Scowcroft and Mr. F. Bindloss got together to discuss the project.

For the first 6 years the course was laid on land close to Gatley Carrs, a local beauty spot, but when this was judged too small, land sufficient for 18 holes was rented in 1891 on the Bradshaw Hall Estate, belonging to the Rev. O.K. Prescott. This venture was never fully pursued and in 1894 the club decided to construct a 9 hole course at Moseley Park Farm with farm cottages being used as a club house. Turves Hall Farm had been used as a club house for the previous year.

In 1894, there was a report of the club's 5th Winter Competition, played in wind and hailstones - 12 players were disqualified for sheltering! J.H. Milne with a net 84, won the 1st sweepstake, C.D. Milne 85 was second. Mr. H. Moseley 97, won the silver medal and C. Hopkinson 88, the bronze medal.

In 1895 occupation was entered into at the new course at a rent of £75 a year. All the club meetings were held at the Cheadle Literary Institute and recorded the first professional, a man named Barlow, at 15 shillings (75p) a week.

The subscriptions in 1907 were 2 guineas with a 3 guineas entry fee. The following year, members planned to buy the course if the price did not exceed £2,500 and promises from Committee members totalling £1,100 were immediately secured - unfortunately the owner was not prepared to sell! The club finally signed a new lease in 1910, the rental having doubled to £150 a year - offset by a sheep grazing lease for £25!

The playing side of Cheadle Golf Club was flourishing and the first matches were arranged with Bramhall Park in the summer of 1914, but then came the War.

For the 1885-86 football season, less clubs were supplying the press with their fixtures, especially the association teams. However, there was a larger increase in new football clubs than rugby. According to F.A. rules, the football season ran from 1st September to 30th April.

The original **Hyde Football Club** was formed in **1885** and is probably best remembered for the all time record F.A. Cup defeat of 26-0, when playing at Deepdale v Preston North End, just 2 years later in 1887. This is still a record score for a competitive match in England - unlikely to be broken!

Hyde originally appear to have worn white shirts and blue shorts. The club began at Walker Fold on the old Hyde Rugby field and also played on a pitch off Mottram Road. Hyde F.C. later went to Townend Street, before moving to the present Hyde United ground at Ewen Fields in 1906, after merging with

Earliest Known Photo of a Rugby Match

An argument during a game in the early 1880s

Hyde St. George's, who played in the Lancashire Combination. Hyde folded in 1917, in view of the demands of the First World War.

Newton Heath L &Y R (later Manchester United) travelled to the South of Manchester to play Levenshulme in 1885, followed by entertaining on their own ground a game v Macclesfield - a 3-3 draw.

**Bramhall Cricket Club** was established in **1886,** on the same site as their present ground. Imagine yourself batting on the 'Queensgate square', the ground open on all sides to fields and hills - bearded gentlemen fielding alongside well-muscled, broad-chested youths, an old black and white pavilion providing a picturesque focal point beyond the boundary. Such would have been Bramhall CC in the early years, for the team would have consisted of farm workers with a sprinkling of Stockport and Manchester business men.

Like so many other villages, it was only the opening of the Manchester, Stoke-on-Trent, London Euston railway line which brought wealthier families to Bramhall and resulted in the many fine houses now situated in the area around the ground.

In 1911, the Honorary Secretary, Herbert Johnson, negotiated for £110 the purchase of a field adjoining the present tennis courts - sadly a familiar tale, that of financial hardship, prevented the buying of this second ground!

A curiosity of these days lay in the playing of bowls across the cricket square and was remembered later by an old Life Member of the club, Lindsay Johnson. He joined as a 10 year old in 1916 and after his playing days continued to serve as the 1st X1 umpire. It was always advisable to bowl after tea when Lindsay was umpiring, as he grew rather excited when the bar opened at 7 p.m. and almost any appeal, however dubious, was answered with his raised finger!

Lawn Tennis was reported for the first time in September 1886 - a local match was South Reddish v Cheadle. The Reddish club won by 10 sets or 67 games to Cheadle's 2 sets or 36 games.

In 1887, the Cheshire F.A. introduced a Cheshire Junior Challenge Cup for 2nd and junior teams to be played in April. An entrance fee of 5s (25p) per team, split into 4 districts: Chester, Macclesfield, Northwich and Crewe.

The summer of 1887 saw Cheshire play cricket against the mighty Lancashire at Cale Green before a crowd of 500, scores: Lancashire 199, Cheshire 66 and 40 for 1 at close of play. Cheshire faired better, shortly afterwards v Staffordshire: Cheshire 259, Staffs 109.

Association football was now rapidly growing in the Stockport area - clubs playing in the 1887-88 season included: Hatherlow (Romiley), St. Thomas, Heaton Norris Olympic, Heaton Norris Wanderers, Lancashire Hill Rovers, Reddish, Edgeley Association, Portwood Wesleyans, Brinksway Rovers, Disley, Edgeley Royal Oak, Romiley, New Mills and New Zealand Wanderers (played at Turncroft Lane).

By the summer of 1888, there was a Stockport Lawn Tennis Club, who were playing Macclesfield with 5 players in each team. Stockport were victorious: Winning 15 Sets to 4 or 112 games to 51.

The Cheshire Junior Football Cup was now in operation, the only club representing this area was Marple, drawn against Macclesfield Swifts. The nearest club in the Senior Cup being Bollington, who were playing Crewe Alexandra.

The Canadians were regular Lacrosse visitors to our shores, and part of their 1888 tour played a match v Manchester & District at the South Manchester Club before a crowd of 5000: Canadians winning 6-1. The local lacrosse teams playing then were: Mauldeth (Heaton Chapel), Heaton Mersey, Withington, Stockport and Didsbury.

Hockey reports appeared in the press for the first time in the 1888-89 season: Sale v South Manchster, Timperley v Kersal, Alderley v Timperley and Bowden Cricket & Hockey v Bowden Hockey Club.

Although there was now a rapid growth in association football clubs, there were still plenty playing rugby around Stockport: Mill Street (Hazel Grove), Stockport Great Moor, Stockport Free Wanderers, Hall Street, Stockport, Edgeley (Cheadle Road ground), Victoria Rangers, Cheadle, Sale, St. James (Heaton Norris Recreation ground), Hazel Grove Wesleyans, Old Garden Boys (Dialstone Lane) and Stockport Athletic (Nangreave Road).

**One of the first ever Rugby matches played under Floodlights, took place at Cale Green in December, 1888:**

**FOOTBALL BY GASLIGHT**

**'A football match was played at Cale Green, Stockport, on Thursday evening under conditions similar to those by which the thousands engaged on the Ship Canal are able to work at night. The ground was illuminated by the Wells patent light. This is an invention which needs some explanation. There is a circular air-tight tank standing about two feet high, from the top of which rises a tube which can be lengthened to any height. At the end of this tube is a burner. In the tank is placed oil, which by means of compressed air is forced up the tube. On arriving at the burner the oil passes in a thin stream through rings and is converted by a certain process into gas, which only needs the application of a light to give out a strong flame of great illuminating**

power, equivalent to 4000 candles.

Messrs Wallwork and Co., of the Union-bridge Iron-works, Manchester, the sole makers of this patent, are very well known in the hatting world by reason of their hatting machinery; therefore the new light is of peculiar interest here. The patent is in use by night at the Stockport viaduct works, and it has attained a national importance by lighting up the way of ships on the Suez Canal. It was through its use at the viaducts that it came to be applied in such a novel fashion on Thursday night. Since the viaducts have been in progress several accidents have occurred, rendering hospital assistance necessary, and it is in order to make some return for this assistance that the football match was organised by those in charge of the works for the benefit of the infirmary.

Most willingly the members of the Stockport Football Club lent their assistance, and the arrangements were entrusted to a joint committee, consisting of Messrs H. Farrington, R. Cox, G. Ritchie, J. Holt (members of the football club), H. Bennett, C.P. Gates, H. Stephens and Mr. J. Marks. Twelve of the patent burners were placed around the ground, making it almost as light as by day, and others were fixed at the entrance gates. A portion of the grand stand was covered in, and boarding to stand upon was laid round some portion of the area - a wise precaution, tending to preserve warmth in the extremities. The general effect when spectators to the number of about 5000 were present was novel and striking.

The whole air was luminous, as at a fire, and faces seen across the ground stood out clearly from the dark background. The faces of a row of youths sat on the hoardings forming the boundary looked like suspended illuminated globes, the other parts of the bodies being nearly indistinct. There was little or no shadow, as from the electric light, and an absence of glare, but there was this drawback, that the gas made a continuous rushing sound like escaping steam. This, of course, is a matter of no moment to a body of men at work, and will hardly be noticed by them, bit it somewhat mars the pleasure derived from a football match, and during moments of suspense, when the spectators are breathlessly watching some critical part of the game, it strikes harshly on the ear. The majority of the spectators on Thursday were, however, too intent watching the game to notice even this, and apparently forget all about it after the first five minutes.

The teams which competed were a fifteen chiefly composed of players in the Stockport Football Club and a fifteen got together by Mr. T. Lees. It was hoped the Mayor would have been able to kick off, but he sent an intimation that he could not possibly be present, and the honour fell upon Mr. Frank Sykes, who was amongst the occupants of the grand stand.

The kick-off took place at half-past seven, and the match terminated about half-past eight, the result being: T. Lee's team, one goal and four minors;

Stockport, two tries and one minor.

FOOTNOTE: The first attempt at an Association game under lights was in 1878 at Bramall Lane Sheffield, by electric power - the second followed 3 weeks later at the Kennington Oval, London.

**Offerton Lacrosse Club** were founded in **1889** and played at various grounds in the area. Though not one of the most successful sides in the history of the game, they were one of the most sociable and friendly clubs! Over the years, the club had its ups and downs and travelled around Stockport in what can only be described as a 'Nomadic' existence. Offerton eventually found a permanent home at Poynton.

An early match traced was in the 1893-94 season, an emphatic victory of 8-1 v Rochdale. As the Lancashire team turned up late, the match was reduced to two '30s'. In 1895-96, Offerton Lacrosse were promoted to the Northern League Second Division, having won the 3rd Division by one point from Monton. By the turn of the century, Offerton had topped League 11. In season 1900-01, the club were playing at the 'windy outpost of Church gate' (Rectory Fields). This was the site where cricket had been staged in the first half of the 1800s.

**Stockport Lads Club** was established in **1889**, when its premises were built on Wellington Street, Stockport (still there) - costing the grand sum of £2,748. The club's memorial stone was laid that year by the Mayor of Stockport, Joseph Leigh, who was to become actively involved in later years as a trustee.

They were playing football at Hempshaw Lane in 1892 and very quickly produced 3 sides, the 1st team thrashed Stockport Albion 10-0 that year,

This was the first club of its kind in the town and given its population, membership quickly swelled with hundreds of lads paying the 1d. weekly subscription - by 1896, the club had recorded over 7,000 names on its registers. When in 1900, the trustees published a review of 10 years work, they reflected on the organisations joint aims of:
'Improving the physical fitness of the boys, which is much in need in Stockport'
And
'Providing opportunities for companionship'
The report also stated how local men of business and good intention contributed to the club. Men such as T.E. Norris, Arthur Styles, John Fletcher and H. Morley joined club founders like S. Moorhouse and Charles Neville in providing sound support both financial and practical, which would see the club establish itself as a firm fixture in the life of young people in Stockport for generations to come.

The Lads club was, in its early years, considered above all-else to be a sporting and athletic club in nature - other activities like draughts, chess and singing were also offered.

Stockport Lads Club Football Team 1911-12

Stockport Lads Club Gymnasts 1909

71

Trustee Martha Bardsley granted £550 in her will in 1902 and club founder T.C. Norris, granted £2,000 to the club in 1909. Mrs. Bardsley's donation went to adding a new Gym at Wellington Street and Mr. Norris's allowed the club to purchase a 4 and a half acre playing field at Hempshaw Lane (their current site). While football and cricket had been activities since 1891, the playing field allowed them to flourish and to continue to improve the sporting skills of members.

Stockport Lads Club's most frequent public face was the gymnastics' team. The addition of a gym had greatly enhanced an already vital programme - from 1900 to 1905, the team had won 4 of the first 5 'Inter Club Gymnastics Competitions. The club would proudly and capably demonstrate its talents to the public of Stockport and Manchester, and featured as a main activity on camping expeditions. The idea of a club camp came to life in 1907 at Allithwaite, near Grange and became a tradition nationwide. Camp would provide young people with the opportunity for holiday time, that would not otherwise be open to them - Prestatyn and Deganwy were the regular centres.

Davenport Harrier's Club organised a run from the 'Duke of York', Heaviley. The 'Hares' were Messrs. J. Lomas and W.H. Lomas, who started with bags (paper trail) at 3p.m. and were pursued at 3.10 by 8 runners from the slow pack, followed by 3 faster runners, 10 minutes later. The trail lay along the main road, Sugar Hall Lane, Woods Moor, Norbury Moor and Bramall Hall. 'Most of the runners wore their new costume which looked very striking'.

Stockport Social Club took part in their 28th cycling run to Disley. Cheadle Cycling Club had a road race from Lymm to Lostock Gralam (Northwich) and back to Mere.

There was now a Stockport Swimming Club at the new baths at St. Petersgate - an Annual Gala took place before the Mayor and Mayoress plus 3 other Councillors in October 1889.

A good example of the basic conditions for early sport: 'Edgeley Rugby club played at Salford v Islington Rangers ground, a brickfield and were told to undress in a hollow in the field. The Edgeley captain Mr. G. Brown thanked those who told him but declined playing under such conditions'.

**Wilmslow Golf Club** was one of 28 golf clubs founded in the UK in **1889** - three of them in Cheshire, the other two being Disley and Macclesfield. From the outset, there were close connections with the St. Anne's Golf Club - later the Royal Lytham and St. Annes Golf Club - from which the founding members were drawn.

It was Lowe, that club's professional, who was engaged to lay out Wilmslow's first 9-hole links, located on land now the home of Alderley Edge Golf Club and the later 18-hole links. Wilmslow originally played to the Rules of Golf used by Lytham and St. Anne's, but towards the end of 1891 adopted 'the Rules of Golf of the Royal and Ancient Golf Club of St. Andrew's'.

On 27th November 1902, the club completed the lease of 101 acres of land with dwelling house and farm buildings at Pownall Brow Farm, Great Warford - this remains the club's home to this day. The original land plus some additions having been purchased by the Wilmslow Golf Company Ltd. For £7,500 in July, 1910. The first changes to the original layout were made by Sandy Herd, born in St. Andrews and winner of the 1902 Open at Hoylake - who in 1910 made alterations to the 12 holes on the far side of the brook.

The *Stockport Advertiser* started showing the forthcoming sporting events, a typical list from January, 1890:

## SATURDAY'S FIXTURES

### FOOTBALL
### RUGBY

| Clubs | Where played |
|---|---|
| Altrincham Albion v Mona Rangers | Altrincham |
| Cheadle Juniors v Hazel Grove A | Cheadle |
| Hazel Grove v Higher Blackley | H. Grove |
| Heaton Mersey v Rhodes | Rhodes |
| Levenshulme v Cheetham Hill | Levenshulme |
| " 2nd v " 2nd | C. Hill |
| Sale v New Brighton | Sale |
| " 2nd v Owens College | Fallowfield |
| Stockport v Blackley | Blackley |
| " 2nd v Blackley 2nd | Stockport |
| Stockport St. Clement's v Brindle Heath | Stockport |
| Stockport Free Wanderers v Mossley | Mossley |
| " Free Wanderers 2nd v Edgeley | Stockport |
| Wilmslow v Flixton | Wilmslow |
| Wright's v Offerton 2nd | Offerton |

### ASSOCIATION

| | |
|---|---|
| Cheadle Heath v Crewe Excelsior | Crewe |
| Bollington v Buxton | Buxton |
| " 2nd v Langley | Bollington |
| Edgeley v Longsight | Longsight |
| Heaton Norris v West Manchester Swifts | Manchester |
| Heaton Norris 2nd v " " " Reserve | H. Norris |
| Hollywood v Failsworth | Failsworth |
| Knutsford v Hurdsfield Rovers | Hurdsfield |
| Macclesfield v Chester St. Oswald's | Chester |
| " 2nd v Beswick | Macclesfield |
| Stockport North End v Marple Brabyn's 1st | Stockport |
| Stockport St. Thomas' v Droylsden | Droylsden |
| " 2nd v " 2nd | Stockport |
| Stratford v Manchester North End | Stretford |
| Tiviot Dale v St. Mery's | Stockport |
| " 2nd v Bollington Cross School | Bollington |
| Vernon Rovers v St. Mary's Swifts | H. Norris |

### LACROSSE

| | |
|---|---|
| Heaton Mersey v S. Manchester | Heaton Mersey |
| " 2nd v " 2nd | Withington |
| " 3rd v " 3rd | Withington |
| Urmston v Harpurhey | Urmston |

### HARRIERS

Davenport - Northern Counties C.C. Championship, Ashton-under-Lyne

**Stockport Association Football Club** started in 1890 and took the town's name at the same time as Stockport County and first played at Adswood, probably on the ground vacated by Stockport Rugby Club a few years earlier. For season 1892-93, the club had moved to the much improved facilities at Cale Green and played in the Manchester League.

This Stockport team were soon strong enough to enter the Cheshire Senior Cup and only lost 2-1 v Northwich Victoria (then in the Second Division) at Cale Green. Stockport had a very impressive list of fixtures v Rotherham Town (Rotherham United), Gainsborough Trinity (joined League Division 11 in 1896), Stalybridge Rovers, Leek and Nantwich.
By 1895-96 season, the Stockport Association had left Cale Green and moved to Poplar Grove (part of Edgeley Park). The club soon went downhill, only playing local football opposition, before folding.

Most people associate Cale Green Sports Ground only as a venue for Cricket and Lacrosse. When Stockport Rugby Club left the cricket ground in 1891, there was a 2 year experiment to play Association Football on the same part of the site. In the 1891-92 season, there were major football matches of the period played there: In the semi-final of the Cheshire Senior Cup, Northwich Victoria defeated Macclesfield 3-1, in front of a crowd of 4,000.

In the Final, Crewe Alexandra beat Northwich 3-1, and attracted a gate of 10,000 (2500 travelling by train from Crewe) - surely the largest crowd for any sporting event up to then in the town. There was a grandstand and temporary stands in place for the game, but little or no terracing, and it makes you wonder how many people had a clear view!

The trial period for football at Cale Green, with the expenses of professionalism, made the effort unremunerative and was discontinued. This part of the land was then let to the 4th Brigade Cheshire V.R. as a general Recreation Ground - the club hoped!.

Stockport County also played on the cricket ground in 1893 v the renowned Blackburn Rovers, then a Division 1 side who had already won the F.A. Cup 5 times. Maybe County wanted a more prestigious ground for the match - a crowd of 4,000 saw the Lancashire team win 3-0.

Two of the first cycling clubs in the town were the Stockport Social Cycling Club, which staged events on a Thursday and Saturday, between April and October in 1890. The Heaton Norris Bicycle Club operated March - October. Cycle shops called Adams had premises in St. Petersgate and Heaton Lane, selling second hand bicycles from 45s (£2.5p) and new Safety's for £7.10s, £9.10s, £10.10s up to £16.16s, Tricycles from £4.

The first ever report of Golf was featured in October 1890. On their own course, Disley defeated Macclesfield by 12 holes, with 7 golfers in each team.

The number of souls living in Stockport in 1892 amounted to 76,253. As the population expanded, so did the number of organisations catering for the different tastes and interests of the individual.

Clubs for football, cricket, tennis, rugby and lacrosse had been started in Stockport and in Heaton Moor itself, so why not a golf club?

**England's oldest Golf Club, Royal Blackheath** dates back to at least **1608** and was unusual for its time being located inland. However, it did not spark off a rush to build other courses. There was no other until 1818, when what is now known as Old Manchester came into being, again inland. The next English course with its first links, Royal North Devon at Westward Ho! Founded in 1864 - the first in Cheshire was the Royal Liverpool club at Hoylake, which was founded in 1869 and hosted the Open Championship of 1897 and 1902.

When courses began to grow in England in the late 1860s and early 1870s, most were inland and these early courses seemed blind to the design features of typical links courses - often of a crude nature.

Early clubs in the Stockport area soon followed: Cheadle 1885, Disley 1889, Wilmslow 1889, Heaton Moor 1892, Marple 1892, Bramhall Park 1894, Mellor and Townscliffe 1894 and Romiley in 1897.

In the late 1700s and early 1800s, Heaton Moor was a moor and mainly farmland. An open aspect gave views to the North towards Manchester and to the South down to Stockport town - to the west of Peel Moat fields the moor stretched down to Burnage Lane and beyond. Farms marked on the old tithe maps carry names which are still in use today - Norris Hill, Green Lane and Lea Gate. Even the names of some of the fields are remembered, New York Field was where York Road is today.

The railway line to the South was opened in 1840 by the then Manchester and Birmingham Railway Company, later to become the London and North Western - with the railway became the beginning of the development of Heaton Moor. The area was served originally by Heaton Norris station, then in 1852 the opening of Heaton Chapel station encouraged much activity by builders. Manchester families began to move from the city areas, building homes near the station on Heaton Moor Road and on new roads opening off it.

**Heaton Moor Golf Club was the first in Stockport**, founded on the evening of March 23rd **1892**, when a group of 12 Victorian gentlemen met at the Conservative Club in Heaton Moor. The chairman

The first clubhouse of Heaton Moor Golf Club in the 1890s

was Mr. Thomas Thornhill Shann, magistrate, local and county councillor, who was to serve for 2 years as Lord Mayor of Manchester and in 1905 to be knighted by King Edward V11 during a Royal visit to Manchester.

The Lea Gate farm and land were sold in 1780 to John Birch, who had been the surveyor of the Manchester to Stockport road - earning his money from the toll gate midway between the 2 towns. Fields in the Mauldeth Estate like Briarfield, Plantation, Hurstfield etc were under the tenancy of one Edmund Wright in 1848 and were part of the land which was eventually the first 9 holes of the golf course.

From the start of the club until 1959, the land was leased from Lord Egerton of Tatton via 2 sources - local tenant farmers and the Hospital Board, which later became the Ministry of Health. Unlike now, with property all around the course, in 1892 it was a joy for the golfers amid open farmland. However, this rural setting had its disadvantages too, because of the agreements which gave local farmers the right to graze their animals on the course!

Mauldeth Hall itself was built in 1839 by Mr. J.C. Dyer and later sold to Mr. Wright whose executors, in turn, passed it to the Ecclesiastical Commissioners in 1854 as a residence for the first Bishop of Manchester, enclosed in 40 acres of land. It was subsequently sold and converted to a hospital for incurable diseases.

The Hall has been an integral part of the club since its foundation in 1892. In this year, the hall had

moved out of private ownership to become the home for a charitable institution, the Northern Counties Supplementary Hospital for Chronic and Incurable Diseases. Apart from organising special events like concerts and other entertainments and the traditional visit by club members on Xmas Day, various competitions were played to raise money for the hospital.

Peel Moat is located within the course - locals and golfers have assumed the land was once the site of a Manor House. It is listed as a site of historical antiquity and comes under the auspices of the Society for the Protection of Ancient Buildings whose representatives visit the area for inspection. 'The site is thought to have been a stronghold surrounded by a moat into which the valuables of the neighbourhood gentry were carried during the Civil War. Cromwell is believed to have sacked and destroyed it.....the site is described by 19th century sources as having a square fortified tower...'

Heaton Moor Golf Club limited membership to 55, and fixed the subscription at one guinea (£1.05) a year. It was agreed that the laying and general management of the greens be left to the Captain, Mr. Glover.

In the first year, score cards were sent to every member. The gentlemen were required to complete 3 to establish a handicap.

The first Clubhouse consisted of a tent bought for £2 10s! In 1893 a Pavilion was bought for the sum of £54 12s 6d complete with a veranda and a small hut at the back to be used as a dressing room!

A man named Thompson was engaged as a gardener for day and a half and later for 2 days a week at 9s. if he looked after the greens.

The first Lady members were elected in May 1892, only a month after the start of the club - 12 Ladies are named in the minutes of the general committee. Initially, it was agreed to limit the Lady members to 25 - increasing to 30 the following year. In September 1894, the membership limit was increased to 50 with the proviso that no more new members should be admitted unless they were either wives, daughters or sisters of members. A pavilion for the Ladies was added in 1898.

As early as 1893, the adoption of a club coat was approved: scarlet with green facings, collar and cuffs at a price of 30s. (£1.50)

The club's social calendar provided a pleasant background to the golf, winter and summer. The 'end of season' supper dance first took place in February 1893 - tickets 5s (25p), ladies 3s 6d. No band was mentioned, but the Orchestral Society were thanked for their services.

In December 1894, the tradition of a dinner was established. In those days the event was for gentlemen only because it was held in various public houses: 'Chapel House', Heaton Chapel and in 1898 the 'Albion', Burnage, where 44 dinners were served at 5s (25p) a head.

The early members were very competitive, playing matches against most clubs in the area - Withington, Bury, Marple, Hyde, Rochdale, Urmston, Fairfield, Bramhall, Trafford, Timperley, Worsley, Cheadle and nearest neighbours the Anson Club.

With all this travelling to other courses, it is no surprise the club approached the Midland Railway for cheap fares from London Road Station (now Piccadilly) plus cheap taxi fares from Heaton Chapel station to the club.

Heaton Moor Lady Golfers in 1900

## HEATON MOOR GOLF CLUB
### Cash Account for the Year ending March 7th, 1903

### RECEIPTS

|  |  |  |  |  | £ | s | d. |
|---|---|---|---|---|---|---|---|
| To Balance of Cash in Bank, March 25th, 1902 |  |  |  |  | 3 | 14 | 3 |
| " Subscriptions:- |  | £ | s. | d. |  |  |  |
|  | **Members** | 204 | 4 | 6 |  |  |  |
|  | **Ladies** | 16 | 5 | 0 |  |  |  |
|  | **Juniors** | 2 | 2 | 0 |  |  |  |
|  | **Visitors** | 2 | 1 | 6 |  |  |  |
|  |  |  |  |  | 224 | 13 | 0 |
| " Entrance Fees |  |  |  |  | 51 | 9 | 0 |
| " Locker Rents |  |  |  |  | 10 | 15 | 0 |
| " Caddies Fees |  |  |  |  | 8 | 7 | 7 |
| " Bogie Cards |  |  |  |  | 7 | 3 | 9 |
| " Cards and Sweepstakes |  |  |  |  | 9 | 9 | 3 |
| " Profit from Annual Dinner |  |  |  |  |  | 10 | 8 |
| " Bank Interest |  |  |  |  |  | 14 | 10 |
| " Ladies Committee, Donation from Tea Profits |  |  |  |  | 5 | 0 | 0 |
| " Rules Sold |  |  |  |  |  | 2 | 8 |
| " Buttons Sold |  |  |  |  |  | 2 | 0 |
| " Refreshments Account Sales |  |  |  |  | 95 | 3 | 9 |
| " Balance due to Bank |  |  |  |  | 3 | 14 | 5 |
|  |  |  |  |  | **£421** | **0** | **2** |

### EXPENDITURE

"

|  | £ | s. | d. |
|---|---|---|---|
| By Rent ... ... ... ... ... ... ... ... ... ... ... ... | 100 | 0 | 0 |
| " Wages ... ... ... ... ... ... ... ... ... | 142 | 11 | 4 |
| " Sand, Cinders, Manure, & c. ... ... ... ... ... ... ... | 5 | 11 | 10 |
| " Grass Seeds ... ... ... ... ... ... ... ... ... ... | 2 | 13 | 0 |
| " Repair, Wire, Oil, Tools, & c, (including extension to Pavilion) | 54 | 13 | 10 |
| " Printing and Stationery ... ... ... ... ... ... ... ... ... | 9 | 15 | 11 |
| " Cleaning Pavilion ... ... ... ... ... ... ... ... ... | 4 | 14 | 1 |
| " Fire and Burglary Insurance Premium ... ... ... ... | 2 | 0 | 0 |
| " Club Mementos and Prizes ... ... ... ... ... ... | 9 | 0 | 3 |
| " Subscription to 'Mauldeth Hospital' ... ... ... ... ... | 2 | 2 | 0 |
| " " 'Gold Illustrated' ... ... ... ... ... | 1 | 6 | 0 |
| " Postages ... ... ... ... ... ... ... ... ... ... ... | 3 | 8 | 10 |
| " Bank Charges ... ... ... ... ... ... ... ... ... ... |  | 11 | 4 |
| " Provender (Fodder) for Horse ... ... ... ... ... | 6 | 11 | 1 |
| " Rent of Room ... ... ... ... ... ... ... ... ... | 1 | 1 | 0 |
| " Hole Tins ... ... ... ... ... ... ... ... ... ... ... | 1 | 15 | 2 |
| " Keys ... ... ... ... ... ... ... ... ... ... ... ... | 1 | 13 | 0 |
| " Boot Scraper ... ... ... ... ... ... ... ... ... ... |  | 13 | 6 |
| " Golf Flags ... ... ... ... ... ... ... ... ... ... |  | 13 | 6 |
| " Sods ... ... ... ... ... ... ... ... ... ... ... ... | 3 | 12 | 2 |
| " Tables ... ... ... ... ... ... ... ... ... ... ... | 1 | 7 | 0 |
| " Registration Fee, New Act ... ... ... ... ... ... ... |  | 5 | 0 |
| " Sundries ... ... ... ... ... ... ... ... ... ... ... | 3 | 13 | 1 |
| " Refreshment Account Purchases ... ... ... ... ... ... | 60 | 4 | 10 |
| " Refreshment Sundry Accounts ... ... ... ... ... ... | 1 | 2 | 5 |
|  | **£421** | **0** | **2** |

Audited and found correct,
**WM. REID THORNBURN,** (Auditors
**FRED W. HALSALL,**                    **THOMAS CHESTER,** Hon. Treasurer

March 9th, 1903

In 1905 the course was increased to 18 holes, using part of the Mauldeth estate, taking in land down to Burnage Lane. The services of Mr. George Low of St. Annes-on-Sea was brought in to advise on the laying out of the new course. A quotation for a green of 12 yards square was £6 - only the best sods to be used!

Also in this year, a larger pavilion was purchased from Victoria Park Tennis Club - 42ft long x 24ft wide and made of wood with a slate roof. A price of £35 was agreed plus a further £60 for removal and re-erection.

The first entry in the Suggestion Book in 1905 from B.H.B. Eldridge, suggested that either bamboo or iron rods be used for flagsticks, so that the flags could be seen at distance - the bamboo rods were ordered immediately!

In 1908, permission was given for the Ladies to join the Ladies Golf Union (Fee £2 2s.) and in 1911 to join the Manchester and District Golf Association (Fee £1 1s.). The playing subscription then was £1 1s. and non-playing 10s 6d (55p).

Further land was acquired and another 'new' course and clubhouse was opened in March 1913 by the past captain and first ever Secretary Mr. R. Scholes.

The First World War saw the 16th and 17th fairways used by the Cheshire Volunteer Regiment (Stockport Battalion) to parade and drill on! A major shock followed just before the war ended - the takeover of land near the firm of Crossleys for the building of an aeroplane factory. This meant that the course was sadly to return to 9 holes. There was a claim for compensation but there is no record if it was ever paid!

Following many years of 'friendly' cricket matches, Leagues were now starting to appear - one of the first being the North Derbyshire and Stockport League in 1892. Some of the clubs taking part: West Gorton, Hazel Grove, Stockport Great Moor, Compstall, and Strines.

Another early League was the North Cheshire Cricket Combination, with teams e.g. Hyde Chapel, Bugsworth, New Mills Primitive, Gorton, Bredbury and Haughton Dale.

On the 13th August **1892,** a group of men including Robert S. Shepley met and resolved that a **golf club** for **Marple** be formed. In the early 19th century, Mr. Shepley, a young Glossop man, purchased a parcel of land in Marple. On part of it he built Rhode Farm Mill for spinning cotton and the rest he let out as a farm. The mill became known locally as Shepley's Mill and is now an industrial estate.

Robert S. Shepley was the club's first Captain and the President was his grandson. He inherited the mill and farm, including large areas of land in Marple, Hazel Grove and Torkington, along with considerable wealth. The industrial revolution led to the creation of a wealthy class of people like R.S. Shepley, who found themselves with leisure time for such pastimes as golf.

Land to lay down a course together with a site for a clubhouse was required - a suitable location was found adjacent to Woodfield Farmhouse, which itself became the clubhouse. Over the years, many changes have been made to the original 9 hole golf course.

The first mention of Marple Golf club in the press was in 1894 - C.H. Roth was winning the monthly medal with a score of 121 less 25 - 96.

In view of the strong rugby presence in the town, in 1892, there was the introduction of the Stockport & District Junior Rugby Union Challenge Shield. The trophy was supplied by R. Higginbotham, Johnson Street, Higher Hillgate - valued at 15 guineas. It was played for by 'A' teams of clubs in the Stockport Junior Rugby Union.

A 'new' team were playing in the East Cheshire & District League in **1892-93**, named as the club of old -'**Heaton Norris**'. Some of the players had played for the original side Heaton Norris Rovers (Stockport County) in the 1880s: Whittle, Simpson, Hockenhall and Kelly. Initially, their games were staged at Green Lane - maybe some extra income for County!

By season 1899-1900 Heaton Norris were based again at the 'enclosed' 'Ash Inn' ground, Manchester Road, where the original team had once played. They had become a premier 'junior' club and were playing in the Stockport & District League, defeating Macclesfield Reserves by 3-1. Another notable win in this campaign, was a 5-0 victory v Buxton.

Several new local football leagues were in operation for season 1892-93. One of the 'rare' occasions that local Leagues were included was in November:

### STOCKPORT & DISTRICT ASSOCIATION FOOTBALL LEAGUE

|  | P | W | L | D | Goals F | A | P |
|---|---|---|---|---|---|---|---|
| Disley | 7 | 6 | 1 | 0 | 21 | 13 | 12 |
| Stockport Swifts | 5 | 5 | 0 | 0 | 38 | 4 | 10 |
| Christ Church | 6 | 4 | 1 | 1 | 32 | 3 | 9 |
| Denton Wanderers | 5 | 4 | 1 | 0 | 26 | 4 | 8 |
| Reddish Olympic | 7 | 3 | 3 | 1 | 23 | 18 | 7 |
| Stockport Lads' Club | 8 | 3 | 4 | 1 | 20 | 21 | 7 |
| Heaton Norris Juniors | 6 | 2 | 4 | 0 | 11 | 12 | 4 |
| Hazel Grove | 6 | 2 | 4 | 0 | 15 | 23 | 4 |
| Mellor | 10 | 2 | 8 | 0 | 14 | 55 | 4 |
| Denton Rovers | 8 | 1 | 6 | 1 | 10 | 57 | 3 |

### EAST CHESHIRE & DISTRICT LEAGUE

|  | P | W | L | D | F | A | P |
|---|---|---|---|---|---|---|---|
| Bollington | 4 | 2 | 0 | 2 | 16 | 7 | 6 |
| New Mills | 3 | 2 | 0 | 1 | 11 | 7 | 5 |
| Leek Wasps | 5 | 2 | 2 | 1 | 17 | 13 | 5 |
| Heaton Norris | 4 | 2 | 2 | 0 | 8 | 11 | 4 |
| Macclesfield Swifts | 3 | 1 | 1 | 1 | 9 | 7 | 3 |
| Fenton | 2 | 1 | 1 | 0 | 8 | 4 | 2 |
| Buxton Rangers | 4 | 1 | 3 | 0 | 5 | 14 | 2 |
| Stockport Swifts | 3 | 0 | 2 | 1 | 6 | 17 | 1 |

## NORTH CHESHIRE LEAGUE

| | P | W | L | D | F | A | P |
|---|---|---|---|---|---|---|---|
| Denton Lads' Club | 7 | 5 | 1 | 1 | 36 | 13 | 11 |
| Hyde St. Thomas's | 7 | 3 | 1 | 3 | 24 | 18 | 9 |
| Dinting Albion | 8 | 3 | 2 | 3 | 28 | 23 | 9 |
| Hyde Borough | 5 | 4 | 1 | 0 | 24 | 11 | 8 |
| Throstle Bank | 7 | 3 | 2 | 2 | 21 | 18 | 8 |
| Glossop North End | 6 | 4 | 2 | 0 | 13 | 18 | 8 |
| Hatherlow | 8 | 2 | 5 | 1 | 36 | 31 | 5 |
| Compstall | 5 | 2 | 2 | 1 | 12 | 11 | 5 |
| * Dukinfield Onwards | 5 | 2 | 2 | 1 | 18 | 19 | 4 |
| Marple | 1 | 0 | 0 | 1 | 1 | 1 | 1 |
| Hadfield | 4 | 0 | 3 | 1 | 5 | 15 | 1 |
| Glossop Olympic | 7 | 0 | 7 | 0 | 7 | 47 | 0 |

*\* Dukinfield Onwards have had one point deducted for playing an ineligible man*

**FOOTNOTE:** In just 6 years time Glossop North End were in League Division 11. A team with the name 'Swifts', was usually a club's 2nd team.

**Disley Golf Club** was started in **1893**, with the course being designed by James Baird. It must be one of the highest locations in Cheshire for a golf course, providing a dramatic landscape, with magnificent views over the Pennines and Cheshire plain.

Land was initially rented from a farmer and all the stone walls on the course caused a bit of a problem! Quite a few of the early members broke away from the club, to help establish Stockport Golf Club. Over the years, the club has staged prestigious events on both a local and national scale.

The Stockport Football Association were formed at a meeting at the Stockport Lads' Club, which was to be their headquarters for many years to come, on March 14th 1893. The proposer of the resolution was Mr. Booth from the Christ Church club, and the seconder Major Sydney Coppock: 'That the Stockport & District Charity Association be formed, and that the rules submitted as passed by the English Association be approved'. When the Association had been formed,

Major Coppick presented the Shield to the committee, with the stipulation that it be competed for annually, and must not become the absolute property of any club.

The following clubs were elected members of the Association at the same meeting:- Brinksway Rovers, Brookfield Rovers, Christ Church, Edgeley, Heaton Norris Albions, Heaton Norris Juniors, Hope Hill Athletic, Hope Memorial, Lads' Club, Levenshulme, Reddish, St. Peter's Recreation and St. Thomas's Recreation.

A second general meeting was held in November, and the number of clubs of the Association had increased the membership to 21.

Another new sport to be reported on in 1894 was Chess. A match was staged between Stockport Christ Church v Edgeley with 6 players in each team. Of the games finished, Christ Church won by 3-2.

**Mellor & Townscliffe Golf Club** came into being in 1920, when the golf clubs at **Mellor (1894)** & **Townscliffe (1908)** merged. In 1745, John Wesley, the famous Methodist Minister, stood on what is now the 10th fairway and described the view that stretched before him as 'Paradise'. Nearly 150 years later, the first holes were laid out on the very same land and Mellor Golf Club was underway.

The Mellor club's first 'Golf House' was in 2 rooms of Clough Farm. Mr. Joseph Taylor and his brother William of Tarden Farm, tenant farmers, leased most of the land on which the early holes were constructed. The 'stewardess' Mrs. Taylor, was initially paid on a corkage basis - Beers and spirits 3d per dozen, soft drinks 2d per dozen, until 1902 at the General Committee Meeting, when a Golf house Charter was introduced:

Opening of new Clubhouse of Mellor Golf Club in 1908

## TERMS OF TENANCY
**Club to be open 10 a.m. to 9 p.m.**
**That the rooms be closed every Friday**
**£12 per annum to be paid for use of fields and 2 rooms**
**£2 for the green keeping**
**One clear day's notice to be given for lunches except bread and cheese or eggs; teas to be ordered by members before going out to play; All food ordered to be paid for.**

This formal agreement cleared the way for the club to become legitimate in its sales of alcohol and tobacco and it became registered under the Licensing Act later that year.

An attempt to raise subscriptions from 10 shillings (50p) to £1 per annum at the A.G.M. of 1905 was strongly resisted by the members! A compromise was reached - members pre-dating 1.10.05 still paid 10s., newcomers paid the increased fee. Children were allowed on the course, under adult supervision - with a strict rule that they should not 'hinder or interfere with the orderly and desired progress of any male member' - they were banned at weekend.

The development of the land had attracted the attention of the Urban District Council and rates paid to the landlords were rising. In 1906, 11d. was paid in rates for the 'Golf House'. Mr. Jos. Taylor became Green-keeper at a wage of 24s. (£1.40) per week, and his wife's corkage rate became a 10% commission on all sales.

The Lady Members had to be kept in check - they were becoming too much of a power in the club! A rule was added, denying them attendance at the A.G.M. and establishing their lack of voting rights! Then their hours of play were restricted! In 1910, they were allowed to form the Mellor Ladies G. C. - in effect a Ladies' Section.

The first moves were now being made to improve clubhouse facilities. After the A.G.M. of 1907, builders were quoting on alterations to Clough Farm, including a locker room - a price of £87 15s without lockers. Discussion turned to a new structure on a separate site, a pavilion. A design was produced and approved by members and a cost of £119 was accepted. A bank overdraft was negotiated and the committee were soon ordering changes - a veranda £13, front gable £5 etc, pushing the price to a total of £155 10s 8d. It was opened in September, 1908, having taken a mere 3 months to complete.

In this year, the ladies had use of a small wooden hut and access to rooms in Clough Farm. The new pavilion did not bring much advantage - a 'small' room was allocated for their use - after protest a W,C, was provided in what was nothing but a cupboard!

To help pay for the new club house, entrance fees increased to £3 3s. for men and £1 10s for ladies -

annual subscriptions also doubled.

In 1909, an advert was placed in the *Manchester Guardian* for a Professional and a Mr. Hardman was employed at 18s (80p) per week and began in 1910 - he only lasted 3 months! The next big development, was extending the course to 18 holes in 1914 with a loan of £500.

The Townscliffe Club had developed from a meeting of 30 people in January 1908 at the 'Midland Inn', Marple Bridge. By February that year, land was leased from Mr. William Jowett together with a clubhouse - he was a wealthy man, a property and mine owner, who farmed at the top of Townscliffe Lane. The course was laid out on the hill slopes from the end of the lane around Townscliffe Farm and up to Mellor Church - signs of old greens or tees are still visible today. The house used at the clubhouse is again privately owned, known as Townslciffe Cottage.

The course was 9 holes and the bogey (par) was set at 72. The membership grew quickly in the first 12 months and numbered 140 - 78 men and a high proportion of ladies at 49. In 1909, a Professional /Groundsman was employed at 18s. per week. To play with the pro. cost 1s (10p) for 9 holes and 1s. 6d for 18 - lessons were 1s. per hour.

It was not until the formation of a Ladies' Section in 1910, that there a hint of unease arose with male members. 'Ladies divots' - the Captain and Secretary drew the committee's attention to the large number of divots after their play on Wednesdays. It was decided to post a notice in the Ladies' clubroom 'to *draw attention to this serious matter*'!

Cash flow problems came to a head in 1913 - the club could no longer afford a professional. There had been money problems from the start - only a credit balance in 2 of its 12 years! The balance sheet showed a shortfall of £95 against an annual income of £220 and the club folded after 1919.

There were only a few cricket clubs playing in leagues. In the summer of 1894, here are some of the teams playing 'friendlies': Reddish, Great Moor, Phoenix, Norbury, Edgeley Loco Shed, Brinnington, Cheadle Wesleyans, Cheadle Hulme, Stockport Congregational, Lancashire Hill, Reddish Vale, St. Peter's (Edgeley), Stockport Lad's Club and St. Mathew's (Edgeley).

**Bramhall Park Golf Club** started life when 40 men sat down in the billiard room of Benjamin Ashwell's Bramhall residence on 8th October **1894** and saw no reason why they could not construct a golf course - for which they had neither land nor funds, within a month! They agreed to form a club with an entrance fee of £1 and a similar figure for an annual subscription.

Attractive clubhouse for Bramhall Park Golf Club in the 1890s

80

Marl Field, at the corner of Park Road and Ravenoak Road, was rented for £30 per year from a local farmer. On the 10th November, 4 gentlemen played the first round of golf on a rough but recognisable 9-hole course.

Bramhall Park Golf Club was born, with 75 members and plans for a rustic pavilion where members could meet and save the wear on Mr. Ashwell's carpets! Ladies 'may be permitted to use the links on payment of 10s 6d. per annum, but not on Saturday afternoons, match or medal days'.

By April 1895, the pavilion and links were formally opened and fees were increased to one and a half guineas. Refreshments included a cup of tea for 6d. and chops or steaks with bread and butter served for 1s 6d.

As the turn of the century approached, the club bought a horse for £5, and in 1903 leased a further 19 acres, allowing the course to be extended by 1905. A new clubhouse on Ravenoak Road was built in 1910, complete with a telephone!

The Great War saw the Bramhall Park Golf Club in decline as members served in the forces and 60 head of cattle grazed the course.

**Cheadle Cricket Club** (now Cheadle Kingsway Sports Club) was formed in **1895**. The early history of cricket in Cheadle is wrapped in the mists of time, but we do know that there were 2 earlier clubs: Cheadle 'Gentlemen' and Cheadle Olympic, who played on Cheadle Green, on the old Cricket Field in Massie Street, later used by Cheadle House School, and on the former Race-course on Manchester Road.

The 2 clubs were merged in 1895, under the presidency of James E. Platt, Esq., of Bruntwood. The club took over the tenancy of the present ground in High Grove Road and soon erected a pavilion, which with later extensions, served for many years. The names of Mr. John Alcock, Mr. George Alcock, Mr. Walter Bennison, Dr. John Godson, Mr. (later Sir) Alan Sykes, Mr. W. Thornton and Dr. Wilson, appear in the records at that time as important members of Cheadle Cricket Club.

Fixtures with many well-known sides brought the club into prominence in district cricket circles, and finances, though fluctuating, were kept sound by the help of donations from good friends, chief of whom was the President, Mr. Platt.

The best known of the cricket professionals, employed a few years later, was Sam Brown, the Cheshire County cricketer, who was with the club from 1906 - 1911.

The outbreak of the War, soon reduced the number of members available for matches - it is recorded that by the end of 1915, over 75% were serving their country. After an attempt to carry on had proved unsuccessful,

it was decided that cricket should be given up, but that the tenancy of the ground should be kept in anticipation of happier times to come!

The Lacrosse sports reporter went under the name of 'Sparrow in the Net'. Listed below, taken from his news column, are the final league tables in the 'golden age' of lacrosse for the Northern League for 1895-96 season:

### FIRST DIVISION

| | P | W | L | D | Goals F | A | P |
|---|---|---|---|---|---|---|---|
| Cheetham | 14 | 12 | 2 | 0 | 111 | 38 | 24 |
| South Manchester | 14 | 10 | 4 | 0 | 104 | 63 | 20 |
| Albert Park & Didsbury | 14 | 9 | 4 | 1 | 110 | 62 | 19 |
| Stockport | 14 | 9 | 4 | 1 | 75 | 55 | 19 |
| Heaton Mersey | 14 | 9 | 5 | 0 | 68 | 49 | 18 |
| Urmston | 14 | 3 | 10 | 1 | 64 | 98 | 7 |
| Owens College | 14 | 1 | 12 | 1 | 37 | 110 | 3 |
| Liverpool | 14 | 1 | 13 | 0 | 27 | 111 | 2 |

### SECOND DIVISION

| | P | W | L | D | F | A | P |
|---|---|---|---|---|---|---|---|
| Eccles | 15 | 11 | 1 | 3 | 84 | 29 | 25 |
| Birch | 15 | 11 | 3 | 1 | 70 | 30 | 23 |
| Chorlton-cum-Hardy | 15 | 9 | 5 | 1 | 82 | 46 | 19 |
| Blackley | 15 | 9 | 6 | 0 | 55 | 51 | 18 |
| Harrogate | 15 | 7 | 5 | 3 | 41 | 38 | 17 |
| Prestwich | 15 | 6 | 9 | 0 | 14 | 42 | 12 |
| Rochdale | 15 | 2 | 12 | 1 | 25 | 59 | 5 |
| North Manchester | 15 | 2 | 13 | 0 | 26 | 83 | 4 |

### THIRD DIVISION

| | P | W | L | D | F | A | P |
|---|---|---|---|---|---|---|---|
| Offerton | 14 | 12 | 2 | 0 | 106 | 16 | 24 |
| Monton | 14 | 11 | 2 | 1 | 72 | 23 | 23 |
| Newton Heath | 14 | 10 | 4 | 0 | 42 | 20 | 20 |
| Burnage | 14 | 7 | 6 | 1 | 63 | 58 | 15 |
| Heywood | 14 | 6 | 8 | 0 | 34 | 55 | 12 |
| Oldham | 14 | 4 | 10 | 0 | 27 | 53 | 8 |
| Bolton | 14 | 4 | 10 | 0 | 31 | 63 | 8 |
| Heaton Moor | 14 | 1 | 13 | 0 | 27 | 106 | 2 |

### FOURTH DIVISION

| | P | W | L | D | F | A | P |
|---|---|---|---|---|---|---|---|
| Cheadle Hulme | 12 | 12 | 0 | 0 | 111 | 13 | 24 |
| Didsbury Park | 12 | 8 | 3 | 1 | 67 | 50 | 17 |
| Old Hulmeians | 12 | 8 | 4 | 0 | 60 | 30 | 16 |
| Failsworth | 12 | 4 | 7 | 1 | 29 | 53 | 9 |
| Ashton | 12 | 4 | 7 | 1 | 23 | 55 | 9 |
| Marple | 12 | 2 | 9 | 1 | 16 | 61 | 5 |
| Christ Church | 12 | 2 | 10 | 0 | 20 | 68 | 4 |

The *Cheshire Daily Echo* sponsored the 'Echo Charity Cup' for local cricket. Permission was given by Stockport Cricket Club for their Cale Green ground to be used for the final in April 1897 between Brookfield Rovers and Christ Church. Admission was 3d and Boys 1d, the proceeds in aid of the Stockport Infirmary.

There were still few Hockey clubs in Stockport by 1897-98 season. The nearest 2 teams results being: Wilmslow 2 South Manchester 2 and Moss Side A 4 Timperley B 2.

The history of **Romiley Golf Club** began in **1897** and started life as the Woodley and Romiley Golf Club. The district was little more than a group of hamlets: Greavefold, Barlowfold, Goosehouse Green, Lane Ends, Butterhouse Green, Hatherlow, Harrytown, Crossmoor (centre of Romiley) - with a total population of 6,000. Goosehouse Green was at one time an 'Extra Parochial Place', an island in the middle of the parish, without the right to attend the Parish

Romiley Golf Club Ladies Medal 1906

- Above picture - Back row M. Crosland, Mrs R. Syddall, Miss M. Syddall, Miss M. Hollingworth, Mr A. Hollingworth. Front row Miss F.L. Woodall, Mrs M. Crosland, Mrs F. Hampson, Mrs A. Smith, Mrs A. Hollingworth, Mrs J. Buckley

Church and, more importantly, not under any obligation to pay rates!

The club was instituted at a meeting on the 29th July, 1897, when Mr. J.E. Lees, of Birch Vale House was appointed Captain, Mr. C.E. Redfern, Treasurer and Mr. L. Conrad Hartley, Secretary. The members numbered 70 gentlemen and 30 ladies. Scarcely any of the ladies played and comparatively few gentlemen - an entry of 12 for a medal competition was remarkable!

The first ground, rented from several tenant farmers, was an area of 31.5 acres, lying to the north of Salters Lane (now Werneth Road) to Mock Beggars Farm (now Hillside) and the footpath leading to Werneth Low - players had a severe climb up the side of Werneth Low! It wasn't long before the club had disagreements with the animals roaming around, which led to weekly rows with the farmers. Also members found the steep slope of the course unsuitable for golf.

In less than a year, the club moved to a new piece of relatively flat ground behind Goosehouse Green, off Barlow Fold Road, Romiley. The club, though heavily in debt owing to money wasted upon the Salters Lane Course decided to build a pavilion. Members were asked for special subscriptions which included the right to make wives subscribers. A total of £214 was raised, and in April 1899, the Pavilion was opened. Later that year, it was decided that the ladies should form their own committee to arrange competitions for the Lady Subscribers.

John Lees, a solicitor, who was appointed Captain, had played golf before moving to Romiley in 1882. He met the 3 times Open Championship winner Harry Vardon, who recommended a young Jersey professional, Thomas Helier Beck, in 1900 - just 17 years old!
In 1905, ladies became members of the club, the original 'Subscribers' being wives of members. The Ladies Section now had the right to admit any lady for membership, as very few wives had joined.

The original course had been rather crude in its construction, having only tees and greens - the fairways cropped by the sheep! There was a need for a longer course, with an improvement in its design - more land was leased and the new course was designed and constructed. Charles Le Chevalier, as Professional and Green-keeper, was responsible for approving the final layout and construction of the 1909 course. The new 9 hole course was opened by the Captain Elect, Dr. Blades, in July 1909.

In 1914, a 21 year lease was agreed on field 124, as was the lease for 2 further Hudson fields (an area covered by the present 3rd and 8th fairways). The War had commenced and the proposed extension to the 9 hole course to embrace field 124 had to be postponed and let for grazing.

In the past we have witnessed cricket matches between 'Gentlemen' v Tradesmen, Men v Women and now Doctors v Solicitors:

**CRICKET**
**INTERESTING MATCH IN STOCKPORT**
**"PILLS" v "QUILLS"**
**'This annual willow wielding encounter between the medicos and interpreters of the law of Stockport, was commenced on the Stockport Cricket Ground, at Cale Green Park, on Wednesday, in overcast, but very sultry weather.**
**There was a good attendance of visitors, guests, etc., who thronged the terrace in front of the pavilion, the fair sex largely predominating. As viewed from the Railway end, the many coloured dresses of the ladies, all shades mingling and blending together, formed a pleasing picture - the appearance might almost be described as that of a large bouquet of varied tinted blossoms.**
**The magnificent Reed Band of the 4th V.B. Regiment was present under the experienced conductorship of genial Bandmaster Fletcher, and rendered pleasing selections of music all afternoon, which did a great deal towards brightening and enhancing the general proceedings.**
**The men were of course in uniform, and very well they looked, too. Afternoon tea was served in the pavilion during the interval between innings......'**

For the record the scores were: "Pills" 90, "Quills" 101 for 4 wickets - I don't think this idea of bands playing throughout cricket matches would go down too well at Lords!

By 1898, Chess had become popular enough for a Cheshire Challenge Cup Competition to be organised. Two matches featured: Stockport 1½ v Sale 6 ½ (8 in a team) and Hazel Grove 1 v Hyde 6 (7 in a team).

**Romiley Cricket Club** was founded just one year later than the golf club in **1898,** on an area of land on Birchvale Farm, the very same site as today. This was used for a few years as a small cricket ground, although it fell into disuse. In the early spring of 1912, a group of enthusiastic cricketers met together to try and reinstate cricket in Romiley. At first games were played on the Recreation Ground at the bottom of Sandy Lane - nowadays Romiley Park.

However, it was obvious to everyone that this was a solution that could not last and later in the same year, the club finally managed to acquire possession of the land at Birchvale Farm. The wicket was cut with hand shears and the first pavilion bought for £6!

In these early years, the club raised money via a series of gala days - often including a cricket match against some of the Chairman's, (Mr. J.C. Fallows) friends, including J.T. Tyldesley, E. Tyldesley, Herbert Sullivan and the great Learie Constantine. These days were supported by the well-known cricket writer, Sir Neville Cardus.

In 1914, many of the club's young cricketers were sent to fight for Her Majesty's Forces in the Great War - of these, 6 men made the ultimate sacrifice: Thomas Ashton, Norman D. Howarth, John William Lundy, Andrew Bernard Smith, Richmond Morgan Smith and Tom Watson.

A cricket match in the summer of 1899 featured teams consisting of Tradesmen v Assistants at Cale Green. There were 12 players a side, scores: Tradesmen 98, Assistants 58.

Bowling had grown from clubs playing each other, to villages in opposition. A match was staged at the 'George & Dragon', Cheadle - Cheadle (281) v Romiley (251).

A group of enthusiastic and optimistic ex-public schoolboys living in and around Heaton Moor held a meeting in June **1899** - it was decided to form **Heaton Moor Rugby Union Football Club**.

The first ground was a rented field on Peel Moat Road, with rather primitive changing accommodation at the Chapel House Hotel on Wellington Road North. Regular fixtures were difficult to obtain, as there were only a dozen clubs in the whole of Greater Manchester - now there are well over 50. For their first ever fixture, Heaton Moor (including the 4 Royle brothers) turned out in a black and white strip on Saturday, 23rd September 1899 v Manchester Athletic Club in Fallowfield (6 years earlier in 1893, an F.A. Cup Final had been played there). The first victory came in the next match v the 3rd Lancashire Fusiliers on the 14th October 1899.

Steady progress was made, so that by 1903, Heaton Moor was able to turn out a Second XI - thanks partly to the folding of their first opponents Manchester Athletic. Two of these former M.A.C. members were later to serve the Moor with distinction. H.S. Johnson was President of Lancashire County R.F.U. from 1928-30, while Fred Jagger was to be Club President for 18 years between 1934 and 1952.

The move to a new ground on Parsonage Road in 1906, a new headquarters at the Plough Inn, Heaton Moor Road and the introduction of their current colours, ushered in the club's must auspicious era.

In the years up to the outbreak of World War 1, the fixture list was extended to include Birkenhead Park, Broughton Park, Kendal, Liverpool, New Brighton, Preston Grasshoppers, Sale and Waterloo on this side of the Pennines - Headingley, Otley and Sheffield on the other. Travel to away fixtures was always by train.

Increased playing strength also meant fielding 3 teams, tours to the Lake District, Bedfordshire and the West Country plus representative honours - Bainbridge, Brown, Burns and Croxford all played for Lancashire, whilst Bainbridge also had the distinction of playing for Midland Counties v the original All Blacks whilst still a schoolboy!

Heaton Moor also hosted the 1908 County fixture between Lancashire and Cumberland.

Off the field, the running of the club was left in the hands of the General Committee, which even selected the teams as the administrative burden was much lighter without a ground and buildings to oversee. Social occasions were a rarity, but an Annual Dance was held at either the Conservative or Reform Clubs. Nevertheless, a certain H. Emmott, who had musical inclinations, composed 3 waltzes after the club colours.

The start of another trend was already noticeable in that members of the same family came to play for the Moor, often in the same side. In subsequent years, Andersons, Baileys, Copleys, Halls, Harrisons, Heaps, Holloways, Clovers, Kelleys, McDonalds, McKays, Nelsons, Thompsons and Tunaleys all played.

In August, 1899, there was the official opening at Hollywood Park of the Open Air Gymnasium by the Mayor before a crowd of thousands. 'Built on similar lines to Heaton Norris Recreation Ground and Vernon Park, there were swings, swinging chains, trapeze, horizontal and parallel bars, vaulting horses, ladders and other requisites for children and older folk'.

Today's equivalent of a walking club in 1900 was called Stockport Field Club. A ramble was organised to Werneth Low via Greave Fold, Romiley, Chadkirk and Offerton. Mr. Hewitt (Hon. Secretary) was the leader. 'Time was pleasantly spent in viewing the extensive landscape from the summit of the Low and the shoulder of the hill at Greave. Field flowers were scarce on the journey'.

Another new sport or pastime to appear on the scene was Draughts. There was evidently sufficient interest to form a Stockport & District Draughts League. A match featured was the Y.M.C.A. (7) v Newbridge Lane (5) with 4 draws - played at the Y.M.C.A. rooms on Wellington Road South.

A Rugby Northern Union County Championship match in 1900-01was between Cheshire and Lancashire. 'The ground at Edgeley Park is perhaps the best Cheshire can boost, a better gate at Stockport than Runcorn, the only other First Division club'. In view of the many Lancashire clubs, it was not a surprise that the score was: Cheshire 0, Lancashire (6 goals, 6 tries) 30 points.

By March 1901, regular golf reports were appearing for monthly medals for clubs: Marple, Cheadle, Didsbury, Timperley Ladies, Bramhall Park, Heaton Moor and Macclesfield.

A month later, the Stockport & District F.A. Cup Final was held at the Mose Rose, Macclesfield, Bollington

# Heaton Moor Rugby Club 1902-03

Back row P. Royle, H. Dean (Secretary), H.G. Small (President), J.D. Russell, G. Woods, F.S. Clarke, T.J. Bowers. Middle row M.R. McClure, J.C. Barnacle, H.B. Marshall (Capt.), J.O. Williamson, W.S. Wallis, W.D. Royle. Front row G. Anderson, E.J. Smith, A. Anderson, F. Williamson, J. Purcell, F.G. Wallis

St. John's v Bollington Cross - it should have been Poynton v St. John's. 'Poynton have assumed the role of spoilt children and refuse to play'....'The executive promptly advertised the final to take place between the two Bollington clubs'.

Bowling had developed to the extent that there was now a Cheshire League. Result of one local match: Cheadle (219) v Hazel Grove (191). There was also the Lancashire & Cheshire Association, which consisted mainly of Lancashire based clubs.

Thomas Wilson of the 'Egerton Arms', St. Petersgate promoted a major sports event held at Stockport County's ground at Green Lane. There were 400 entries from Lancashire, Cheshire and Staffordshire, attracting a large number of spectators.

In season 1902-03, the annual Cheshire v Lancashire lacrosse match was played at Cale Green. This fixture dates back to 1880, with the Lancastrians winning most of the early encounters. In recent times, Cheshire were victorious in 6 of the last 7 games - on this occasion losing by 10-8. The Cheshire team was taken from: Cheadle Hulme, Stockport, Heaton Mersey and Offerton.

The Manchester League was operating for this season, some of the football clubs taking part were: Northwich Victoria, Hyde, Sale Holmefield, Denton and Macclesfield.

The Northern Croquet Championship in June 1903 was held at Alderley Edge - spread over several days. Competitors came from as far away as London, Cheltenham and Cork. There were tournaments for Ladies, Men and Mixed Doubles.

Stockport Cricket Club staged a bowling event for its members at Cale Green, engaged in the Hatting Trade (205 points) v Allied Industries (230). There were 24 members in each team.

Walking contests were proving to be a popular sport in this summer of 1903. The most important one being the 26 mile round trip from Stockport - Macclesfield. There was a committee organised by Mr. G.W. Brown, proprietor of the 'Three Crowns Inn', Old Road, Stockport. The 'checking stations' were the 'Butley Ash', Macclesfield and the 'Orange Tree Inn', Butley. The prizes on offer were: silver lever watch value £2 5s, watch, chain £1 1s, travelling bag, silk muffler, gold centre medal, pipe and case, no cuddly toy!

Another walking event was organised by the L. & N. W. Railway Electrical Works - a circular walk from the 'Hollywood Hotel' - Grenville Street, Chapel Street, Shaw Heath, Longshut Lane, Macclesfield Road to Adlington, Wilmslow, Handforth and Cheadle. The winner was S. Platt in a time of 3hours 28 minutes and 53 seconds.

The meetings of cycling clubs were published for the first time:

| | |
|---|---|
| Stockport Wheelers | : Wincle |
| Stockport Adams Social | : Lymm |
| Stockport Sunday School | : Pickmere |
| Albert CC | : Buxton |
| Heaton Norris | : Pickmere |
| Reddish | : Peover |
| Stockport Al Fresco | : Disley |

The 'Gentlemen' of Cheshire were continuing to play their cricket matches at Chelford in 1903 - they were easily beaten by Old Cheltonians, 251 runs to Cheshire's 72 and 64.

Football in New Mills must have existed since the very early days of the sport. You could say that the area was a smaller version of so many Lancashire towns that produced clubs which were to become founder members of the Football League - many based upon the huge number of mill-workers as in New Mills. Only 3 years after Stockport County were founded in 1883, matches v New Mills regularly appeared in their fixture lists - sometimes defeating the Stockport team! Unlike the Lancashire Mill Town clubs, I doubt if the High Peak outfit would have had the resources to 'import' players down from Scotland!

The first football ground was possibly on the site of the present cricket pitch off Church Road - there was also an early ground by the River Goyt on the South side of the railway viaduct.

The start date for **New Mills Football Club** is accepted as **1903**. This was when the New Mills St. George's team was formed, with their home ground on Millfields - long disappeared under the Ollersett Estate. The side consisted entirely of local players, who changed at the 'Bull's Head' - a now demolished public house, standing near the bottom of High Street. Much of the town was concentrated in this area at the time and St. George's became so successful, that they attracted large attendances on Millfields - often numbering 2 or 3 thousands. Big crowds also gathered on the Hyde Bank bridge to cheer the team back to the 'Bulls Head' after the latest victory! Bad news though in defeat - they were forced to 'run a gauntlet' of Torr Top women, brandishing umbrellas at both players and officials!

In season 1905-06, both the Stockport League and Cup trophies came to the New Mills club, along with the prestigious Derbyshire Minor Cup.

Besides the St. George's team, other local sides began to evolve and several five-a-side teams sprung up - often based on local industrial establishments. These teams competed in various medal competitions and, in 1905, St. George's players George 'Jelly' Allen, Sam Taylor, Sam Marsland, Bill Lomas and his brother 'nowty' Frank won no less than 5 gold medals!

The St. George's Football Club in 1904, a forerunner of the present New Mills F.C.

The Whaley Bridge and New Mills medals competition was a keenly fought contest - one New Mills participant declared he would swim back to the town from Whaley by way of the canal if his team were successful - they were and he did! Many of the competing teams were bizarre in name if not reputation. The Pingot colliers were a pretty venomous bunch, entering a side known as Pingot Stingers. Another famous five-a-side outfit played under the banner of New Mills Flat Ribs - they had a reputation for throwing the opposing centre-forward over his own crossbar if he was challenged unduly!

In 1910, a St. George's player, outside-right Harold Crosswaite, was transferred to Stockport County, who by then were playing in Football League Division 11. He broke into the County team in season 1912-13 and up to 1922-23, went on to make 131 appearances, scoring 11 goals.

After the outbreak of the Great War, the St. George's club was disbanded, but in their brief and illustrious history, they had won almost every honour on offer! Towards the end of the War, the present New Mills team came into existence.

**Hazel Grove Bowling and Tennis Club** were first registered as a limited company on 2nd May **1903**, to commence business on the 22nd May. The objects for which the company was formed:

"To establish and maintain a Club or Clubs at Hazel Grove in the County of Cheshire for Bowling, Tennis and any other outdoor or indoor games."
The initial directors and their professions were:

John Adshead J.P.   - Schoolmaster
Dr. Thomas Moor   - Surgeon
John A. Holland   - Manufacturer
George Lockett   - Schoolmaster
Robert J. Fletcher   - Public Accountant
Joseph Gosling   - Clerk
Ralph Clayton   - Stockbroker
Percy J. Bayley   - Railway Agent
Joseph D. Penny   - Company Director

A prospectus was agreed with a capital of £500, 350 shares were offered for public subscription at £1 each and the remainder reserved for issue later. Land was acquired in Wesley Street for a term of 10 years at an annual rent of £12 4s 8d - the plot fronting the street measuring 77 yards. Plans were drawn up and tenders obtained for the work of laying the green, tennis courts and grounds. The tender was accepted from Tom Park, Davenport Crescent in the sum of £155 0s. 9d. A cart track from Queens Road had to be established to the site for the contractor.

Hazel Grove Bowling & Tennis Club members in their 'Sunday Best' in 1910

A site was agreed for a Pavilion to be built at a cost of £124 10s 0d, followed by a water service by the Council. Subscriptions for a years membership being open to share holders and close relations only! Male members 1 guinea (less 1/- for each one fully paid share held. For a lady member who is a shareholder or the wife, sister or daughter of a male shareholder 5/- (25p) - other ladies 7/6d. Any member may introduce a friend and shall be responsible for their conduct, but no person resident within 10 miles shall be introduced more than 4 times a year!

As membership grew, the club recognised the need for further tennis courts. In 1906, a further plot of land on the south side was added for this purpose. In 1909, a scheme was approved for enlarging the pavilion. The important step of purchasing the land for £550 from Mr. Gelling was completed in 1913. Croquet became so popular, that the players asked for more space! The Bowling section arranged friendly competitions home and away with Victoria and Cale Green Clubs. A resolution was passed in 1913, for the company to be suspended as far as possible for the continuation of the War.

The Stockport & District Football League had a membership large enough to run 2 divisions for season 1903-04. There should have been 14 clubs in each league - 'The record of the Edgeley team has been withdrawn and the whole of the matches expunged from the league'. The Edgeley reserve side, still played in Division 11.

An advertisement for the Alec Watson sports shop in Manchester for cricket equipment:
Bats full size with all cane handle 4s 6d, 5s 6d, 6s 6d, 9s 6d
Cane & rubber handles 10s 6d, 12s 6d, 14s 6d
Balls - club match 3s 6d each or 38s per dozen, special crown match 4s or 24s per dozen, best catgut sewn 5s or 63s a dozen

Another new sport or pastime was taking place by 1904 - Ring Throwing. There was a Cheshire Ring Throwing League in place with a 1st & 2nd division, consisting of 11 pub. teams in each competition. There was also a Manchester Salford & District organisation with a Stockport (South Division) - 9 pubs with 1st and 10 with 2nd teams.

Stockport County's old ground at Green Lane was still being used for football in 1904-05 season. A Stockport & District league match between Hazel Grove and New Mills had to be decided at a neutral venue. The Derbyshire club started the match with only 9 men and not surprisingly lost 4-1.

**Stockport Golf Club** started life at Woodsmoor in **1905** - its most important founder member was George Orme. He was a member of Disley Golf Club, but the stone walls on the course and the fact that the club rented land from a farmer who restricted their activities in improving the course, very much detracted from golf's pleasures. He had the idea of starting a links in the vicinity of Stockport, where George was living at the time.

Land was found off Bramhall Moor Lane to house a 9 hole golf course and a pavilion was bought from the engineering firm of Boulton and Paul - it provided retiring rooms for ladies and gentlemen and smoke rooms and other facilities. When the Davenport club moved to Torkington in 1907, the pavilion was sold to Fulshaw Golf Club for £60. Traces of the original course are still visible on the approach to the railway bridge or seen from a passing train.

All the original committee were members of Disley Golf Club. Orme and many of the golf club members also belonged to the Davenport Club, a business men's social club at Cale Green, still in existence today. Committee meetings were held there and the golf club run from there until 1912. Davenport Golf Club was instituted in December 1905 and golf began to be played at Woodsmoor early the following year. Certainly the full nine holes were in play by that summer. An account in the 'Stockport Advertiser' in July featured the opening of the new pavilion and mentions that 9 holes played twice, were equal to a distance of 3 miles. The course was popular with members - there were 75 original members and that number doubled in 2 years. It was noted that 2 nights 'are devoted to ladies, of whom there is a goodly number'.

With its location in the Bramhall area and the adoption of the name Davenport Golf Club, it was natural to adopt as its crest that of the Davenport family who had lived at Bramall Hall for centuries.

The first general meeting took place in December 1906. Nine ladies were present and they decided to form a Ladies' Committee.

By 1908, membership numbers had risen to 188 gentlemen and 70 ladies - only 12 ladies actually played golf, but they took visitors along to play on Tuesdays. The ladies felt it was time they awarded their own handicaps and no longer to ask the gentlemen to do this!

The Davenport Golf Club was made famous by a ball being driven over the railway by a Mr. Worrall, hitting a locomotive and bouncing on to the course again! At Woodsmoor, the course and its pavilion may have been humble, but they gave the club a start. Development was already underway, not least because the site was at risk from the power of the Freeholder's Company who had the right to take any portion of the course required for building purposes. This risk could affect any golf courses located close to large towns, so there was never any prospect of extending to 18 holes.

Messrs Orme and Hyde were busy looking for land suitable for a good 18 hole course and eventually

The original clubhouse at Woodsmoor

Robert Hyde discovered the land at Torkington - the committee inspected the land and they approved of it. A lease of 21 years with the option of a further 14 years was arranged and future purchase at a later date. An option was taken to extend the term of the lease or to purchase the land freehold for a price of £10,000. Orme and Hyde selected the site for a number of reasons, not least the fact that they could guarantee not to lose the grounds through some future land deals. It was also an open site, with few trees - in many respects it resembled an inland links.

Trees had to be cut down and ditches filled in and many miles of drain pipes laid down - there were then no mechanical shovels, tractors or motor mowers, as today.

About 122 acres were secured from Mr. R. Shepley complete with a farmhouse and outbuildings. The land had formerly been part of the estate of

Farmhouse converted into the first
clubhouse on present site 1900

Torkington Hall, once the seat of the Torkyngton family who had been connected with the estate since about 1200.

Having acquired the land, fields which had been farmed for centuries, the club could begin the construction of its new course. Sandy Herd, one of the outstanding players of his generation, was retained to plan the layout, although the work was carried out by Peter Barrie and a team of 20 men. When he began work on the Torkington course in 1908, Barrie lived in one of the Bosden cottages across the road from the club entrance.

It was at Mr. Hyde's suggestion that the name was changed to the Stockport Golf Club and that it was formed into a company limited by guarantee in 1908, which took over the assets and liabilities of the Davenport Golf Club.

As for the old course at Woodsmoor, when vacated by Davenport, it was part of the land leased from Sir J.E. Barlow by Mirrlees, Watson and Yarvan factory in Glasgow - Mirelees Golf Club survived until 1988.

Sandy Herd had won the 1902 Open Championship at Hoylake, the first important championship to be won using the Haskell or rubber-cored ball. It was suggested that Herd purchased the entire stock of the Haskell ball from the Hoylake professional so that the ball was not readily available to other competitors!

Up to that point, all players had been using the gutta-percha ball or Guttie - the Haskell was much easier to get airborne with the primitive hickory-shafted clubs available. This was not the only advantage, the Guttie, once in the air, behaved predictably on landing - it

Official Opening Day at Stockport Golf Club 1910

H. STOTT    G.A.ORME        A. GASKELL    J. LONGSON    DR J.H.SMITH    R.HYDE.

F. ROBINSON    PETER BARRIE    JAMES BRAID    J.H.TAYLOR    A.BRIGGS.(CAPT)    HARRY VARDON    Alex HERD.    WM JOHNSTON    W.N.BATTERSBY.

stopped dead! The Haskell, however, bounced and rolled on landing.

The farmhouse at Torkington, included in the lease, provided the basis for conversion into a clubhouse with facilities for both ladies and gentlemen - including a kitchen and large dining room. The farm buildings had accommodation for a motor car garage, sheds for bicycles ( a pump was purchased for use by members) and stables for horses - providing for members travelling from a distance.

After some 18 months of intensive work, the new course at Torkington opened on 7th August 1909, with a match between the Captain's side and the Vice-Captain's - some £2,000 had been spent and all the members were impressed at Barrie's creation.

The official opening was on 9th May 1910, when there was a 36-hole better-ball match between J.H. Taylor and Harry Vardon representing England and James Braid and Alex Herd representing Scotland.
The move to Torkington brought new interest to ladies' golf and it reported at the 1910 AGM that there were 117 lady members - unfortunately there were no separate ladies tees.

Peter Barrie had been appointed both Professional and Green-keeper. This was not unusual at this time, and it was also quite common at some clubs for the professional to be expected to help out behind the bar. Club professionals, although expected to be good players and teachers of the game, were not granted

much time off to practise or to play in tournaments. The wage then being 15/- (75p) per week with teaching and playing fees fixed at 2/- (10p) per hour for coaching. An important duty was returning lost golf balls to members, supplementing their modest wage. They were paid 2d for each ball returned!

A letter in 1911 from Miss H. Bancroft complained of the very bad appearance of the sheep on the course. It was arranged that the attention of the farmer be drawn to the complaint!

In June 1912, it was decided to improve the little clubhouse to provide extra locker accommodation. Oil lamps were used to light the various rooms in the clubhouse, but an application was put forward to the council for electricity.

Green staff & equipment c1912

Club Staff of Stockport Golf Club c1912

In September 1914, the House Committee was authorised to reduce the price of gin by 3d a glass, only to put up the price of beer and stout by a halfpenny.

In March 1916, an offer was received from farmer John Holland of Broad Oak Farm of a fee of £80 per year for the grazing of sheep on the course!

It is interesting to look at the prices charged in the Dining Room in 1916:

|  | s | d |
| --- | --- | --- |
| Pot of tea | | 3 |
| -do- with biscuits | | 4 |
| -do- with bread and butter or toas | | 6 |
| -do- with bread and butter or toast, jam & cake | | 9 |
| Eggs extra each | | 3 |
| Plate of cold meat | | 9 |
| Hot lunch | 2 | 3 |

Bar Prices recommended:

|  | s | d |
| --- | --- | --- |
| Mineral waters | | 3 |
| Syphon soda | | 2 |
| Liquers | | 6 |
| Bottled beer or stout | | 4 |
| Perrier | | 4 |
| Cherry Brandy | | 6 |
| Whiskey (small) | | 4 |
| Whiskey (large) | | 8 |
| Brandy (small) | | 5 |
| Sherry or port | | 6 |
| Claret (large bottle) | 3 | 6 |
| Claret (small bottle) | 2 | 0 |
| Champagne (large bottle) | 12 | 0 |
| Champagne (small bottle) | 6 | 6 |
| Cigars | | 4d, 6d, 9d & 1/- |
| Cigarettes Three Castles | | 6d & 1/- |
| Gold Flake | | 4d & 8d |
| Tobacco | | 8d per oz |

In an effort to boost membership, entrance fees were reduced in 1916 and it was reported that 62 men and 22 ladies had joined since this initiative.

One area in which the World War 1 had some impact was public transport, and in November 1916 a Special Committee was set up to look into the cost of providing some sort of transport from the Bull's Head public house in Hazel Grove to the clubhouse - suggesting the possible purchase of a 5-seater Ford motor car with a driver provided from the ground staff.

It was agreed in November 1916 to allow the links to be used for cadet training and early in 1917 a letter

was received from Hazel Grove Council concerning utilising part of the course for the growing of crops. The secretary replied that the land was already let for the grazing of sheep and that was serving the national interest. A visit from the Cheshire Agricultural sub-Committee resulted in the club giving up 12 acres to be sown with oats, later wheat and potatoes.

Bramhall Park Golf Club had opened in 1894, but some 10 years later, there was a feeling that there was a desire for a second golf club in Bramhall. Preliminary investigations took place into land availability, meetings and discussions were held in private, as James Ramsdale forged ahead with plans to bring the dream to fruition.

The reaction to the invitation to attend an inaugural meeting on 3rd May **1905** in the Board School, Bramhall Lane, was disappointing - only 11 people had responded by post, and only a further 22 residents actually attended. However, by the end of the evening, all 33 had stated a willingness to join the proposed **Bramhall Golf Club.**

It was agreed, that if the club was to be formed, the entrance fee would not exceed £2 2s. and the subscription a maximum of £1 11s. 6d. A plan of the 9-hole course, to be laid out on 36 acres of land on part of Ladythorn Farm, occupied by Henry Nield, was submitted by Mr. Ramsdale. Mr Nield agreed to let the land, together with 2 rooms in the farmhouse to be used as club and locker room, for £50 per annum. On 10th May, a second meeting was held, at which a further 12 promises were forthcoming, and on the strength of 45 founder members, it was decided that The Bramhall Golf Club was born.

At the beginning of 1906, it was felt that an Annual Dinner should be investigated - the venue was the Victoria Hotel, Bramhall, and the charge to members and friends 3s. a head - for those wishing to attend the evening after the dinner, the charge was 6d.

It was during the club's first full summer in 1906, that the interest of the local press caused some embarrassment to members as they printed competition scores. To save their blushes, it was resolved that no scores over 90 should be published! In March of that year, Henry Chisholm was dismissed and a Mr. Burgess of Alderley Edge was appointed Club Professional/Grounds-man at a wage of £1 a week, with an additional allowance for rail fares!

During the first full season, Mr. Thomas Rowbotham formally presented a silver cup to be played for - the Rowbotham Cup, still fought for to the present day.

By December 1907, Arthur and Agnes Nield had taken over the running of the farm from Henry, and there was a new arrangement governing the use of the land. The ladies were becoming an increasingly active section, and an additional room in the farmhouse was given to their use - all lady members should attend the AGM.

In January 1908, there were 2 unfortunate incidents - one of Mr. Nield's horses was drowned in the pond near the first green, and shortly afterwards, a member played a shot which struck a lamb and broke its leg, causing it to be destroyed! Mr Nield put in a claim for compensation for the loss of both animals. The club disclaimed liability for the loss of the horse, but agreed to pay £5, which included a gratuity, for the loss of the lamb.

In 1908, the club was thriving, with a growing and enthusiastic membership - the committee found considerable support for the idea of an 18-hole course - a further 3 fields totalling 36 acres were bought from Arthur Nield at £1 10s. per acre and a further field of 10 acres from Mr. Worthington of Poynton. The new 9 holes were open for play by 1st May 1909, and the par for the full course was set at 80.The question of Sunday play was raised, but brought a negative response!

The ladies had an additional competition to fit in during 1908, Captain's Prize - there were 2 prizes on offer - one for ladies with a handicap of 40 and one for those with a handicap of less than 40.

There was some dissatisfaction among members concerning the layout of the course - Alex Herd, the 1902 Open champion was invited to come and play, and offer his expert opinion. He played with the Captain, and went round in 74, expressing his approval of the course. He stated that he had never seen a better or more varied course on the same amount of land - now 72 acres. Mr. Herd, later sent a detailed report of each hole and how it may be improved, with special reference to bunkering.

In October 1909, a letter was read from the National Telephone Company drawing attention 'to the desire of some subscribers to speak to the club on the wires' - it was decided that at present there was not sufficient need to justify a telephone - it arrived 3 years later!

An Open Meeting was held in June 1910 - at which the thorny question of Sunday play was once again raised. To many golfers, the ban imposed by the landlords was a great irritation, although the Council, on its own initiative, had allowed some relaxation of the rules. However, in July, there was a change of heart on the part of the landowners - after consultation with Mr. Rowbotham, it was agreed that play should be allowed on Sunday's between 1pm and 5pm, but that Juveniles should be excluded and the Club Room closed! Because of Mr. Rowbotham's strong connection with the Methodist Church, the course was not opened until after morning service and had to be closed before the bells rang for evening service!

By 1907, there were 7 Cycling clubs in Stockport. Five of them, in the spirit of the suffrage movement, were progressive enough to admit women. Cycling in late Victorian and Edwardian times became a national craze. Models produced by famous cycle manufacturers such as Rudge Whitworth, Sturmey-Archer and the Starley and Sutton 'Rover', allowed the man in the street to enjoy a previously undreamt of local mobility. As H.G. Wells observed in his 1896 novel 'The Wheels of Chance': 'We are all cyclists nowadays'.

In June 1907, the Stockport & District Amalgamated Hairdressers Association held a Sports Day. By kind permission of Mr. Marsland of Woodbank, one of his fields was used for the event. Some of the activities taking place were: 100 yards, ¼ mile, wheelbarrow and for Ladies only - skipping rope, egg & spoon, thread needle and shuttle cock.

**Bramhall Lane Lawn Tennis Club** was founded in **1907.** It has always been a members' club, that celebrated its Centenary recently in 2007 with many special events including a Mid-Summer ball.

Turning the clock back to 1907, when some 28 friends who played regular social tennis on a garden lawn just off Bramhall Lane South, moved their activities to newly laid grass courts in farm fields at the end of, what was eventually to become, Ramsdale Road.

The garden lawn of a house on Bramhall Lane South at its junction with, what is now, Ladythorn Road, is remembered as the point of origin for the club we know today. In 1907, Bramhall Lane South was indeed a lane and Bramhall itself a small village surrounded by farms. One such farm was Pownall Hall Farm, on the opposite corner of Ladythorn Road, later the site of the County Hotel - the first pair of semi-detached houses on Ladythorn now occupies the original garden lawn-cum-tennis court.

The 28 friends moved to what is now Ramsdale Road, at its junction with Carrwood Avenue. There was access to this site via a wide field gate on Bramhall Lane South where it meets Ramsdale Road, and onward by path through grazing fields.

Two grass courts surrounded by wire netting were erected at a cost of £44. A wooden hut was hired for 10s. (50p) per annum to serve as a tool shed, tearoom and changing room combined! These 2 grass courts occupied the land where the end house at 15 Ramsdale Road lies and on what is the practice wall and number 9 court adjacent to the entrance to the club today. The first year's accounts of 1908, showed a loss of £23!

Membership was by invitation only in the early years. Expenditures recorded in the period of the run up to the First World War were:

Mrs. Bertha Irwin of Heaton Mersey,
borrowed the cycle for the photo in 1903

| Bucket | 10 Pence |
| Dozen Tennis Balls | 11 Shillings |
| Prizes | 4 Shillings |
| New Shed/Pavilion | £11 10s. |
| Relaying of grass | £13 |
| Turf Specialist | 2s. 6d. |

A third grass court was added in 1910. Membership dropped from a high of 48 to a low of 22 during the War years.

**Cheadle Football Club** were playing in the Federation league for season 1908-09. The committee had 'high hopes' for the new campaign, 'to be the most successful in the clubs history with an impressive fixture list'. The 'blues' were only defeated twice at home, by Rusholme (Champions) and Poynton, but had a poor away record.

The Cheadle club were fortunate to have a gentleman like Mr. J.H. Davis of Moseley Hall in their midst, Chairman of Manchester United - recent winners of the F.A. Cup. To celebrate the occasion of his team appearing at Crystal Palace, he invited 9 of the Cheadle club committee, the grounds-man and 3 players to watch the game in London. They were given a railway ticket to St. Pancras, 2s 6d stand ticket at the match and 5s for expenses. They all arrived home feeling very tired at about 5 a.m. the following morning!

There were players in their ranks who had previously appeared for Stockport County, Denton, Hooley Hill, Stalybridge and Moseley Moss Side - any previously paid, would now have to revert to strictly amateur. Football in the early years in Cheadle was dominated by Rugby - the Cheadle R.U.F.C. folded some years earlier, like many other rugby teams around Stockport. The association club played on the same ground as the rugby club had done on Wilmslow Road.

The Federation League table results up to March 13 1908-09:

### MANCHESTER FEDERATION

| | P | W | L | D | Goals F | A | P |
|---|---|---|---|---|---|---|---|
| Rusholme | 20 | 17 | 2 | 1 | 62 | 26 | 35 |
| Didsbury | 22 | 16 | 6 | 0 | 63 | 29 | 32 |
| Eccles Borough | 20 | 12 | 5 | 5 | 51 | 29 | 29 |
| Cheadle | 22 | 10 | 5 | 4 | 54 | 32 | 24 |
| Chapel-en-le-Frith | 20 | 10 | 7 | 3 | 39 | 32 | 23 |
| Poynton | 18 | 9 | 6 | 3 | 41 | 40 | 21 |
| Alderley Edge United | 20 | 10 | 9 | 1 | 45 | 47 | 21 |
| Macclesfield | 20 | 9 | 9 | 2 | 32 | 31 | 20 |
| Rochdale | 20 | 7 | 11 | 2 | 37 | 48 | 16 |
| Altrincham | 18 | 5 | 10 | 3 | 32 | 39 | 13 |
| Whaley Bridge | 20 | 5 | 12 | 3 | 28 | 54 | 13 |
| Oughtrington Park | 15 | 6 | 9 | 0 | 26 | 29 | 12 |
| Buxton | 17 | 2 | 13 | 2 | 21 | 45 | 6 |
| Pendlebury | 9 | 2 | 7 | 0 | 17 | 24 | 4 |
| Thornsett United | 9 | 1 | 7 | 1 | 10 | 28 | 3 |

The annual lacrosse match between Cheshire and Lancashire was staged at Fallowfield Athletic stadium. Between the years 1895-1902, Stockport had a very strong team, which reflected in the victories that Cheshire achieved in this period. Now with a weaker side, Cheshire were easily beaten 14-3.

**Stockport Georgians Football Club** was started **1908.** St. George's Church, Buxton Road, had left land in trust for sporting activities - resulting later in football, cricket and tennis being played there. The first competitive football they played was in the Stockport League - the club's initial success followed in the late 1920s.

In the 1870s, it appears that Rugby was played on this site - Stockport Rugby Club and the Crusaders Club. Going back even further, to the middle of the 19th century, one of Stockport's early prominent cricket clubs, Charlestown, was also in the area.

The Stockport & District League had grown to 3 divisions by season 1908-09. The top 3 clubs in Division 11 had finished on level points, making a play off necessary - the winners being the Park Albion club, with Stockport Lads runners-up.

**Fred Perry** was born in a modest terraced house on Carrington Road, Portwood in **1909,** and he started playing tennis at the age of 14. In 1929 he not only made his debut at Wimbledon, but also won the Table Tennis World Championship held in Budapest, Hungary.

He was selected to play for the Great Britain Davis Cup team in 1933 and in the same year won the US Lawn Tennis Association Championship. Fred went on to win Wimbledon 3 years running in 1934-36,

# Earliest Known Photo of a Football Match

'Gentlemen' players of Association Football c1880 - the art of tackling!

resulting in him being made a Freeman of Stockport in 1934 - the year he won the Australian Open title. He died in 1995, aged 85 and remains Britain's greatest ever tennis player, winning 8 grand slams.

The Lancashire & Cheshire Amateur League was formed in 1909. Two local clubs taking part were Davenport and Bramhall. There were 12 clubs in the 1st and 2nd Divisions - 'Only bona-fide amateurs are allowed to take part'.

Hazel Grove, like many areas of Stockport were predominantly rugby strongholds before the association game established a foothold. **Hazel Grove Football Club** possessed a footballer called Harry Parkinson, soon after the turn of the century, who was known by Manchester League clubs and supporters as the 'Demon'. 'He is only young in years, but what he lacks in these he makes up in his tricks, for he appears to have a charm over the ball that many opposing custodians can vouch for. Harry is 21 years old, stands 5ft 3in. and weighs 8st 7lbs.' He had played for Heaton Norris Reserve for one season, scoring 2 goals in a match v Vernon Swifts, stayed on the pitch and played in the first team v Hazel Grove Central, scoring another 3 goals! His scoring record was: 1904-05 32 goals, 1905-06 34, 1906-07 52 (8 hat tricks), 1907-08 21, 1908-09 20 (up to March 13).

The Manchester League was the strongest football competition which included local clubs. Results table up to April 19th 1908:

### MANCHESTER LEAGUE

| | P | W | L | D | F | A | P |
|---|---|---|---|---|---|---|---|
| | | | | | Goals | | |
| Macclesfield | 29 | 18 | 6 | 5 | 77 | 42 | 41 |
| Northwich Victoria | 28 | 16 | 9 | 3 | 68 | 49 | 35 |
| Tonge | 30 | 16 | 11 | 3 | 54 | 45 | 35 |
| New Mills | 29 | 13 | 8 | 8 | 72 | 44 | 34 |
| Altrincham | 29 | 15 | 10 | 4 | 78 | 56 | 34 |
| Hazel Grove | 28 | 13 | 9 | 6 | 58 | 43 | 32 |
| Salford United | 28 | 14 | 10 | 4 | 59 | 54 | 32 |
| Tyldesley Albion | 30 | 12 | 12 | 6 | 72 | 67 | 30 |
| Witton Albion | 29 | 13 | 12 | 4 | 76 | 58 | 30 |
| Sale Holmfield | 27 | 14 | 11 | 2 | 61 | 52 | 30 |
| Ramsbottom | 29 | 12 | 13 | 4 | 60 | 75 | 28 |
| Denton | 29 | 10 | 12 | 7 | 52 | 66 | 27 |
| Hooley Hill | 28 | 10 | 12 | 6 | 56 | 49 | 26 |
| Berrys | 28 | 10 | 13 | 5 | 51 | 51 | 25 |
| Buxton | 29 | 7 | 18 | 4 | 39 | 71 | 18 |
| Newton Heath | 29 | 0 | 26 | 3 | 33 | 100 | 3 |

For season 1909-10, the club were playing on their ground at Grosvenor Street in the Manchester League. An earlier ground was opposite the 'George & Dragon'. A notable victory this season was a 1-0 win against Macclesfield. The previous seasons, Hazel Grove were competing in the Stockport & District League, before moving to the higher standard of football.

The Grove ground was used for the final of the Charity Cup, when Hazel Grove Amateurs beat Edgeley Loco by 1-0, 'The Amateurs fully deserved their victory, playing a clean and scientific game against much heavier opponents'.

Season 1910-11 saw Hazel Grove progress to the 3rd round of the Cheshire Senior Cup, but were well beaten 7-0 by Stockport County Reserve at Edgeley Park. In the summer of 1912 there was a fund raising Athletic Sports Day for the 'Grove', held at their old ground near the 'George & Dragon'. The A.A.A. rules were applied for the day, with accompaniment by the Hazel Grove Silver Band.

A new addition to the football scene in 1909-10 was the introduction of the Stockport Amateur League. By nature of the league's name, one wonders if some players were therefore being paid to play in the Stockport & District League?

The league tables at the end of season 1909-10:

## STOCKPORT & DISTRICT FOOTBALL NOTES BY "ONLOOKER"

### STOCKPORT & DISTRICT LEAGUE
### FIRST DIVISION
FINAL TABLE

| | | | | | Goals | | |
|---|---|---|---|---|---|---|---|
| | P | W | L | D | F | A | P |
| Chapel-en-le-Frith | 16 | 13 | 0 | 3 | 45 | 15 | 29 |
| Woodley | 16 | 9 | 4 | 3 | 39 | 24 | 21 |
| Bollington | 16 | 6 | 4 | 6 | 33 | 23 | 18 |
| Little Hayfield | 16 | 8 | 7 | 1 | 37 | 27 | 17 |
| Burbage | 16 | 7 | 7 | 2 | 32 | 32 | 16 |
| Baker Street Social | 16 | 6 | 6 | 4 | 21 | 27 | 16 |
| Wilmslow United | 16 | 4 | 9 | 3 | 28 | 44 | 11 |
| Waterloo Albion | 16 | 3 | 9 | 4 | 26 | 39 | 10 |
| Hatherlow Social | 16 | 2 | 12 | 2 | 27 | 57 | 6 |

### SECOND DIVISION

| | P | W | L | D | F | A | P |
|---|---|---|---|---|---|---|---|
| Park Albion | 26 | 21 | 3 | 2 | 88 | 22 | 44 |
| Cheadle Lads | 26 | 18 | 6 | 2 | 64 | 44 | 38 |
| Reddish | 26 | 16 | 6 | 4 | 65 | 33 | 36 |
| Reddish Swifts | 26 | 14 | 9 | 3 | 58 | 33 | 31 |
| St. Peter's | 26 | 15 | 10 | 1 | 49 | 41 | 31 |
| St. Joseph's | 26 | 13 | 8 | 5 | 55 | 57 | 31 |
| Handforth Juniors | 26 | 12 | 8 | 6 | 60 | 42 | 30 |
| Cheadle Heath United | 26 | 12 | 11 | 3 | 58 | 50 | 27 |
| Newbridge Lane | 26 | 9 | 12 | 5 | 46 | 55 | 23 |
| Marple Recreation | 26 | 7 | 13 | 6 | 47 | 65 | 20 |
| Baker Street Reserve | 26 | 6 | 13 | 7 | 42 | 59 | 19 |
| Wilmslow Reserve | 26 | 6 | 18 | 2 | 36 | 66 | 14 |
| Portwood Church | 26 | 4 | 17 | 5 | 31 | 60 | 13 |
| Stockport Adult School | 26 | 2 | 21 | 3 | 17 | 89 | 7 |

* * * *

### STOCKPORT AMATEUR LEAGUE
FINAL TABLE

| | P | W | L | D | F | A | P |
|---|---|---|---|---|---|---|---|
| Heaton Mersey | 22 | 18 | 1 | 3 | 67 | 20 | 39 |
| Hazel Grove Amateurs | 22 | 14 | 4 | 4 | 51 | 28 | 32 |
| Social & Temperance | 22 | 13 | 5 | 4 | 43 | 26 | 30 |
| Edgeley Primitives | 22 | 13 | 6 | 3 | 53 | 31 | 29 |
| Cheadle Heath United | 22 | 9 | 7 | 6 | 47 | 40 | 24 |
| St. Matthew's | 22 | 9 | 10 | 3 | 47 | 34 | 21 |
| North Bramhall | 22 | 6 | 9 | 7 | 30 | 34 | 19 |
| Moorside | 22 | 7 | 11 | 4 | 35 | 47 | 18 |
| Hempshaw Lane Wes. | 22 | 6 | 13 | 3 | 39 | 56 | 15 |
| Reddish Green Wes. | 22 | 5 | 13 | 4 | 35 | 62 | 14 |
| Diesel Rovers | 22 | 4 | 14 | 4 | 37 | 64 | 12 |
| Old Hydonians | 22 | 4 | 15 | 3 | 31 | 73 | 11 |

Macclesfield F.C. arranged a prestige football match v Queens Park (Glasgow) over the Xmas holiday period of 1910 - a large crowd saw the game end 1-1.

During the 1910-11 football season, the Stockport League Management Committee had a few problems to sort out at their meeting held at the 'Egerton Arms', St. Petersgate:

A letter was received from the Secretary of Reddish Swifts, 2 players refusing to play when requested. The players failed to put in an appearance and were banned until they turned up! The Secretary was censured for his unsatisfactory evidence! Reddish were fined 5s (25p) for not fulfilling their match v Handforth.

St. Joseph's were reported for a late start and playing 10 men, fined 1s for each offence.

Little Hayfield v Hollywood was a game unfinished, the Hollywood explanation was unsatisfactory - the game to be replayed on cup tie terms.
St. Joseph's v Stockport Junior Conservatives, the match stopped by spectators 13 minutes early - to be replayed.
Cheadle Heath fined 2s 6d for cancelling a game v St. Joseph's on Boxing Day.
Hollywood used an unregistered player and fined 2s 6d.
Park Albion sent in an incomplete result card twice, fined 1s for each offence.

The 1910-11 football season saw the introduction of the Stockport Sunday School League. There were A (10 clubs) and B (12 clubs) Leagues, plus a Junior Division with 12 teams competing.

Cheshire were playing Lancashire in the annual lacrosse match at Cale Green before a good sized crowd. The Cheshire side consisted entirely of Stockport players, apart from 2 Cheadle Hulme men. Cheshire were victorious by 8-7.

Bowling was continuing to be a well loved sport in the Stockport area, a few results:
Davenport v Cheadle Heath (won by 2 points), at 'Jolly Sailor' Hotel
Great Moor v Buxton (won by 1 point)
Compstall 186 v Bollington 254
Great Moor 271 v New Mills 331

Football was still a growing sport and in 1911-12 season, the Reddish Amateur League was underway. It consisted of 14 clubs in surrounding areas of Stockport and Denton.

Many hockey clubs had been founded over the past 20 years, below are the results for a Saturday in January 1912:

| | | | |
|---|---|---|---|
| Cheshire | 5 | Yorkshire | 2 |
| Sale A | 7 | Altrincham A | 1 |
| Bowden | 5 | Oxton | 2 |
| Stockport | 3 | Bury | 0 |
| Timperley | 4 | West Derby | 1 |
| Heywood | 2 | Levenshulme | 2 |
| Sale | 4 | Altrincham | 1 |
| Y.M.C.A. | 7 | Sale College | 1 |
| Kersal | 5 | South Manchester | 2 |
| Stockport A | 3 | Bury A | 1 |
| St. Annes | 5 | Brooklands | 2 |

# Edgeley Football Club in 1902

Back row Heywood*, Worsley*, Suart*, Barrett. Middle row Downes, Hodgkinson*, Pass*, Newton, Chester. In front Millward, Nolan. *Players to later play for Stockport County

| | | | |
|---|---|---|---|
| Northenden | 5 | South Manchester B | 0 |
| Chorlton | 1 | Knutsford | 0 |
| Hyde | 4 | Stockport B | 0 |
| Winnington Park | 5 | Latchford | 1 |
| Ashley | 5 | Cheadle | 2 |

All the above were men's hockey matches, the only ladies' club mentioned in reports, was Davenport.

The final of the Cheshire Senior Cup was staged at Edgeley Park in 1912 before a crowd of 2000. The replayed match ended: Crewe Alexandra 4 Stalybridge 2.

**Reddish Vale Golf Club** was established on April 12th **1912**, when a group of gentlemen met at Heaton Moor Conservative Club to launch the club. No doubt there had been previous discussions and endeavour put into the project to build a new golf club on land owned by the Greg family in Reddish.

Mr. H. Howarth took the chair and N. Rosenburg was elected Secretary, with R. Cooke becoming the first Treasurer. Little was decided at this meeting other than to elect F.W. Reed as the first Captain of Reddish Vale Club.

It was not until August that meetings commenced, held at South Cliffe (club house) and Heaton Moor Reform Club. Considerable time and expertise was devoted to membership, organisation, with the formation of 5 committees namely: House, Greens,

Finance, Handicaps and Rules. Messrs Stockwell, Williamson & Co. were appointed the stock takers, with the wealth of the club lodged with the Manchester and County Bank.

It was soon realised that there was a need to look after the welfare of the members and their guests - after interviewing from a short list of 6, Mr. W.H. Morgan, together with his wife, was appointed Steward and Stewardess at the princely salary of £1 10s. per week until March 1913. The wage would then reduce to £1 per week plus all the profits on catering. The club agreed to provide a maid, whose keep was down to the Steward.

One of the greatest golf course designers of his time, Dr. Alister MacKenzie from Leeds, was engaged by the club. The great doctor achieved greater fame in the years leading up to the early 1930s with his designs at Augusta, Crypress Creek, Royal Melbourne and many others including Pasatiempo where he subsequently died.

The grand house on the land was in a good state of repair but alterations were considered necessary and an immediate decision was taken to pull down the conservatory in order to be able to build a club room. There was plenty of space for a dining room, smoke room, ladies dining room and sitting room, visitors' bedrooms, ladies' club room and locker room Provision for re-decoration and the purchase of items of furniture for the various rooms was approved.

Goal-Mouth Action From A Match in 1891

The year when the referee with whistle & notebook was transferred from the touchline to inside the playing area. Courtesy of the F.A.

In April 1912, Mr. H.J. Redfern was appointed chairman of the Greens Committee and the following implements were purchased:

| | |
|---|---|
| 2 48" Heavy Box Rollers | £21 each |
| 1 24" Hand Roller | £3 9s. |
| 1 32" Hand Roller | £8 |
| 1 42" Horse Mower | £33 15s. |
| 2 Hand Mowers | £5 15s. each |
| Flag Pins/Misc. Tools | £10 |

The cost for an 18 hole golf course would not exceed £120, although the links opened initially with only 5 holes.

By May 96 debentures (bonds) had been applied for together with 33 applications from ladies. June's meeting produced the visitors rules and a green fee of 2s 6d or one round playing with a member for 1s. was considered. A move to allow ladies to introduce a visitor for 1s. was rejected and ladies became subject to the same rules as the men.

July 1912 and the first formal meeting of the golf club at South Cliffe - during this occasion, 52 ladies and juniors were elected as members. A garden party was held to raise funds and it proved to be successful and the fore-runner of many.

In an attempt to stop small boys on the course, the Chief Constable of Stockport was instructed to have a plain clothes officer on duty for the next 2 Sundays, the club bearing the expense. A police constable subsequently returned 3 golf balls, but as the balls could not be identified by any member and the boy had been caught off the course, it was decided prosecution would be futile!

The ladies were also causing problems, because some of them were not keeping to their allotted rooms and some members were of the opinion that the rule should be rigidly enforced and any lady member who persisted in straying should be requested to submit their resignation!

The club was beginning to experience some financial difficulties - the financial statement indicated a surplus of only £19. Various suggestions were made as to the raising of money e.g. by advances on the security of new members share capital and subscriptions. In the end, 8 members agree to loan the club £50 each and others agreed to act as guarantors to the banks.

It was suggested that £1,000 be raised, as well as the £450 required, before the end of June to complete the 16 holes already made, as expenditure was required during the winter to finish the last 2 holes.

At long last, a professional was appointed - he was Peter Rainford and it was stated there had been a marked improvement in the scores by those members who had availed themselves of his services. He also carried out the duties of Head Green Keeper during a period when the club was without one. Concern was expressed at the professional entering the club house - the captain undertook to speak to Rainford about this practice!

There were 544 visitors from August 6th 1912 until July 23rd 1913, even though 18 holes were not yet completed. Membership now consisted of: Full members 142 - Country 9 - Non-playing 4 - Lady Members 110 - Juniors 8. Total 273.

The Stockport & District Playing Fields Society made 4 new Football pitches available for rent at the Highfield Estate at Davenport, complete with dressing rooms.

Football season 1912-13, saw another new league underway, the Stockport Combination - consisting of 3 Divisions, 'A' with 15 clubs, 'B' with 10 and 'C' 12 teams. The first season finished as follows:

### STOCKPORT COMBINATION "A" DIVISION

| | P | W | L | D | Goals F | A | P |
|---|---|---|---|---|---|---|---|
| Cheadle Heath Wes | 26 | 19 | 5 | 2 | 74 | 31 | 40 |
| Avenue Rovers | 26 | 17 | 4 | 5 | 94 | 32 | 39 |
| Heaton Villa | 26 | 18 | 5 | 3 | 84 | 32 | 39 |
| Cheadle Lads Club | 26 | 16 | 8 | 2 | 66 | 38 | 34 |
| Stockport Lads Club | 25 | 15 | 8 | 2 | 54 | 36 | 32 |
| St. Peter's | 25 | 12 | 6 | 6 | 58 | 34 | 30 |
| Edgeley | 26 | 10 | 9 | 7 | 44 | 39 | 27 |
| Hyde Wesleyans | 26 | 8 | 9 | 9 | 55 | 41 | 25 |
| Spring Vale | 24 | 10 | 11 | 3 | 49 | 42 | 23 |
| Alderley Edge Vic | 26 | 10 | 13 | 3 | 57 | 58 | 23 |
| Gee Cross Wesleyans | 24 | 5 | 13 | 6 | 36 | 46 | 16 |
| Portwood Church | 26 | 2 | 19 | 5 | 26 | 55 | 9 |
| Vernon Amateurs | 25 | 4 | 20 | 1 | 34 | 113 | 9 |
| S.S.S. Brotherhood | 25 | 2 | 21 | 2 | 16 | 110 | 6 |

**FOOTNOTE: Owing to several clubs not having sent the results of some of their matches they are not included in the above table.**

The Stockport Union of Conservative Clubs had their own Billiard & Whist League. Teams taking part included: Cale Green, Jennings, Wellington, Brinksway, Victoria and Reddish.

There was a major Bowling event held at the 'Chapel House' Hotel, Heaton Chapel in September 1912 - Amateurs v Professionals. All the well known players from Lancashire and Cheshire taking part.

In January 1913, Stockport Harriers were still holding regular events for their members. The Club Championship started from the 'Bulls Head' Hotel, Hazel Grove. 'Trail lead over a heavy course, the fields being under water, by Mr. H. Openshaw and Mr. G. Hutchins. Hope Valley to Chester Road, returning via Dean Lane and Macclesfield Road, round the course twice. From 16 members competing, 11 completed the full course, the winner was A. Barton in 48 minutes 1 second'. The following Saturday, the race was to start from the 'Egerton Hotel', St. Petersgate.

**Bredbury St. Mark's Cricket Club** was formed in the year **1913**, by the players and officials of the then successful Football Club of the same name- the footballers were playing in the Stockport Sunday School League in season 1913-14. The new project was fostered by the interest and encouragement of Mr. Plant, whose organising ability had already proved to be of great value!

The cricket club decided to rent the field off Werneth Road, their present ground - which had been previously occupied by Greave Cricket Club. The disused playing pitch was still evident and soon restored. The club was immediately accepted into the Stockport and District League. They won the first ever match v Hazel Grove Wesleyans, and went on to win the competition in their first season.

Play continued through 1914 and into the following year, but by then, too many players had left the cricket field for the wider fields of Flanders; work on munitions had claimed others, and activities were suspended. Care of the ground was left in the capable hands of Mr. T.W. Bramall and Mr. Hill.

**Hazel Grove Golf Club** started life in **1913**. The modest first site being some rented farmer's fields at Bosden, Hazel Grove. Following a short tenancy, the members found an alternative venue at Mill Hill, Hazel Grove and 12 months later another move was made, this time to the present course at High Lane. It was then that the club started to establish itself and the membership grew accordingly.

In March 1914, the Stockport Football Association celebrated their coming-of-age (21 years), with a dinner at 'Crossley's Café' in the Market Place. The past winners of the Charity Shield to date were:

1892   *Christ Church
1893   Reddish
1894   Reddish
1895   Reddish
1896   All Saints
1897   Little Moor
1898   Little Moor
1899   Offerton
1900   Christ Church
1901   Edgeley
1902   Edgeley
1903   Edgeley
1904   Reddish United
1906   Hazel Grove Albion
1905   Reddish United
1907   Heaton Norris
1908   Portwood Church
1909   Waterloo Albion
1910   Park Albions
1911   Edgeley Primitives
1912   Hazel Grove C.
1913   Edgeley Primitives
*Winners before the Association was formed*

The monthly meeting of the Stockport League at the 'Egerton Arms' continued to deal with club's misdemeanours in January 1914:

'Chapel F.C. were reported for a late start, and for playing ten men against Compstall Wesleyan F.C. The Chapel secretary explained that owing to one of the players being without distinctive attire the Compstall club objected to his playing, and he was ordered off the field by the referee. The club was excused.

Great Moor Amateurs were also reported for late start on December 20 against Broadstone F.C., and for playing seven men; for playing ten men and for being 60 minutes late against Romiley St. Chad's F.C. on December 27, the match being abandoned after 55 minutes play. For the first offence they were fined 1s, and in the second case fined 2s for the late start, 1s for playing ten men, and the game ordered to be replayed on Cup-tie terms.

India Mill F.C. were reported for failing to turn up against Great Moor F.C. on Boxing Day; and they were ordered to pay half of the referee's fee and expenses and fined 1s. (5p)

Buxton F.C. claimed 5s (25p) from the Brinksway Club for expenses incurred through the latter club cancelling their league match to play a Cheshire Amateur Cup-tie. It was resolved that the Buxton Club be informed that the committee regrets that, owing to the fact that a Cup-tie takes preference over a league match, it cannot grant the claim.

Heaton Mersey Lads' Club F.C. were fined 1s for failing to turn up against Romiley St. Chad's F.C., and ordered to pay half the referee's fee and expenses. The match was arranged for March 28.'

There were however, problems of a more serious nature going on at 2 games reported in the same edition of the *Cheshire Daily Echo,* also in January 1914:

### THE MACCLESFIELD v CHESTER MATCH
### REFEREE MOBBED

**'At the close of the football match on the Moss Rose Ground, Macclesfield, on Saturday, the referee had a somewhat exciting experience. Macclesfield were entertaining Chester in the first round of the Cheshire Senior Cup Competition, and during the game the referee had a number of decisions which the crowd did not consider fair. In one instance particularly the spectators showed great disapproval of the referee's ruling. He had awarded a goal for Chester, which it was contended was an offside one. The referee, after consulting the linesmen, adhered to his decision, to the great annoyance of the supporters.**
**With the exception of a certain amount of barracking, however, nothing untoward occurred**

until at the end of the game, when a number of the spectators "rushed" the ground, chasing the referee and "booing" him as he made his way towards the dressing room. But for the intervention of the police and a number of committee men, the referee might have been roughly handled.

Although he waited until it had gone dusk before he ventured to walk down to the station, he had not got far from the ground before he was observed by a number of the "barrackers" who had evidently awaited his arrival. Several police officers and civilians formed an escort for the referee, who was jeered at and "booed". In a short time he was surrounded by a large crowd, and very soon missiles were thrown. One of the policemen guarding the referee had the misfortune to be hit on the jaw with a potato. The referee, however, luckily escaped injury, and was allowed to remain in the Police Station, pending time for the departure of his train'.

### ROW AFTER FOOTBALL MATCH
### EXTRAORDINARY SCENE AT STALYBRIDGE
### OFFENDING PLAYER ESCAPES VIA STOCKPORT

'The Crewe goalkeeper's (Box) foolish action at the close of the Stalybridge Celtic Cheshire cup-tie with Crewe Alexandra on Saturday led to some exciting scenes at Bower Fold, Stalybridge.

Throughout the whole game the players on both sides were guilty of infusing feeling into their work. When the game was over, and the Crewe players were going to the dressing room Box met Joe Brooks, the Celtic Captain, in front of the grand stand, and, without the least provocation, challenged him to fight. The Crewe man stripped off his sweater, threw it on the field, and attempted to strike the Celtic captain. Fortunately Chorlton and Spittle, the two Crewe backs, prevented a collision.

When Box got to the gate the crowd, which had rushed on to the field attacked him. He was banged in the ribs several times, and struck on the head with sticks. When he got through the gateway he was again assaulted, and with the help of police officers got to the dressing room in an exhausted condition. He was subsequently conducted by a field-path to Hyde, where he took a car to Stockport, and there caught his train'.

In cricket season of 1914, there was still a 'class issue', as the 'Gentlemen' of Cheshire continued playing at Chelford, this game v the 'Gentlemen' of Worcester. The drawn match scores; Cheshire 188 & 136 for 4, Worcester 209 & 238.

The Stockport & District League were to reduce the football competition to one league for season 1914-15. The following clubs taking part: Buxton, Fairfield, Chapel-en-le-frith, Bollington Cross, Bollington United, Wilmslow North End, Poynton Amateurs, Horwich End, Disley and Compstall Wesleyans.

Late in July, on a Saturday summer afternoon in 1914, cricket was being played as usual in the 1st Division of the Stockport & District Cricket League:

| | |
|---|---|
| Reddish Vale 83 | Denton St. Anne's 39 |
| Bugsworth (for 8) 106 | Reddish Aspinal 42 |
| Christy's 96 | Hope Chapel 40 |
| Hazel Grove Wesleyans (for 4) 55 | Denton Christ Church 36 |
| Bredbury St. Marks (for 5) 55 | Denton UMC 47 |

A few days later, War was to be declared.......

# Index

# Bibliography

'THE CHESHIRE COUNTY NEWS'

'STOCKPORT GOLF CLUB ONE HUNDRED YEARS' - Mark Rowlinson  (2007)

'HEATON MOOR GOLF CLUB' 1892-1992 - A.A. GIBBON

'THE OLDEST LACROSSE CLUB' - Tony Malkin (1996)

'STOCKPORT CRICKET CLUB 125 YEARS' (1980)

HISTORY WEBSITES: BRAMHALL, COMPSTALL, DIDSBURY, ROMILEY CRICKET CLUBS, BRAMHALL PARK, HAZEL GROVE, WILMSLOW, CHEADLE, ROMILEY, MARPLE GOLF CLUBS, HEATON MOOR RUFC, HYDE UNITED F.C. (2008)

CALE GREEN PARK - Stockport Metropolitan Borough Council

'POYNTON SPORTS CLUB CENTENARY 1885-1985' (1985)

STOCKPORT CRICKET CLUB BAZAAR HANDBOOK (1893)

'THE STORY OF THE MILLERS' - Martin Doughty (1974)

'STOCKPORT COUNTY 100' - Carole Ann Perry (2000)

'STOCKPORT ADVERTISER'

'CHESHIRE DAILY ECHO'

'STOCKPORT COUNTY A COMPLETE RECORD' - Peter Freeman (1994)

WEST HEATON 1873-1973

'MELLOR & TOWNSLCIFFE GOLF CLUB 1894-1994' - A.G. Smart 1994

'ROMILEY GOLF CLUB THE FIRST 100 YEARS' - Frank Beard 1996

'BRAMHALL LAWN TENNIS CLUB'

HURST HISTORY OF STOCKPORT

# Acknowledgements  & Thanks

I wish to thank the following people for supplying information and also supplying photographs:

Marcus Heap , Stockport County fan

Carole Perry & other staff, Local Heritage Library, Stockport (7 Photographs)

Kay Moore (Librarian) Cheadle Hulme School & Melanie Richardson (School Historian)

Secker & Warburg, 7 John Street, Bloomsbury, London

Robert Hale Ltd., 45-47 Clerkwell Green, London

John Howarth & Steve James, Stockport Golf Club

Pam Bann for her excellent proof reading skills

Margaret Hardman, Heaton Moor Golf Club

Bryan Rendell, Reddish Vale Golf Club

Barry Livesay & team, Stockport Cricket Club

Brian Downer, Bramhall Lane Lawn Tennis Club

Sandra McDermott, Cheadle (Kingsway) Sports Club

Howard Smith, Poynton Sports Club

David Ashworth, Didsbury Cricket Club

Allan Jones, New Mills Football Club

Frank Beard, Romiley Golf Club

Arrow Books Ltd., 3 Fitzroy Square, London

Alan Pearson, Hazel Grove Bowling & Tennis Club

Victor Wright, Mellor & Townsliffe Golf Club

David Gibson, Heaton Norris

Raymond Prior, West Heaton Bowling & Tennis Club

Stewart Helm, Stockport Grammar School (Historian)